Matters of Taste: Food and Drink in Seventeenth-Century Dutch Art and Life

MATTERS OF TASTE

Food and Drink in Seventeenth-Century Dutch Art and Life

DONNA R. BARNES and PETER G. ROSE

With Essays by

Charles T. Gehring and Nancy T. Minty

and Supplementary Cookbook

by Peter G. Rose

Albany Institute of History & Art / Syracuse University Press

LIBRARY OF CONGRESS CATALOGING-IN-PUBLICATION DATA
  Barnes, Donna R.
    Matters of taste : food and drink in seventeenth-century Dutch art and
  life / Donna R. Barnes & Peter G. Rose.—1st edition.
        p. cm.
  Published to accompany an exhibition held Sept. 2002 by the Albany Institute of History and Art.
  Includes bibliographical references and index.
    ISBN 0-8156-0747-4 (pbk. : alk. paper)
  1. Still-life painting, Dutch—17th century—Exhibitions. 2. Still-life painting, Flemish—17th century—Exhibitions. 3. Genre painting, Dutch—17th century—Exhibitions. 4. Genre painting, Flemish—17th century—Exhibitions. 5. Cookery in art—Exhibitions. 6. Cookery, Dutch. 7. Cookery, Dutch—History. 8. New Netherlands—History. I. Rose, Peter G. II. Title.
    ND 1393.N43 B37 2002
    758'.4'09492074747—dc21   2002009565

Composed in Rialto type
Printed by Everbest Printing Company
Book design by Christopher Kuntze

Manufactured in China

The Albany Institute of History & Art wishes to thank the following
for their support of *Matters of Taste*:

Matthew Bender IV

Phoebe Powell Bender

The Bender Family Foundation

Mrs. Marjorie W. Kenney

Cultural Tourism Initiative, a project of the Arts & Business Council Inc.
and the New York State Council on the Arts

KeyBank

RABO-Bank International

Sotheby's, Inc.

McNamee Lochner Titus & Williams PC

Allison C. Bennett

The City of Albany

The Netherland-America Foundation

Consulate General of The Netherlands, New York

Alan P. Goldberg

Earl B. Wing

Roberta D. Corbett

Lois Kocis

Pariseau/Sacramone Family

Excelsior College

Barbara Braden

William A. & Greta H. Wagle

Mark LaSalle

Arnold A. Krueger

Donna R. Barnes, Ed.D., who co-curated the Matters of Taste exhibition with Peter Rose under the auspices of the Albany Institute of History & Art, is professor of education at Hofstra University. Since 1990, she has collaborated with Rose on several projects concerning seventeenth-century art. Dr. Barnes has curated three exhibits at Hofstra's Emily Lowe Gallery: *People at Work: Seventeenth-Century Dutch Art* in 1988; *Street Scenes: Leonard Bramer's Drawings of Seventeenth Century Dutch Daily Life* in 1991; and *The Butcher, the Baker, the Candlestick Maker: Jan Luyken's Mirrors of Seventeenth-Century Dutch Daily Life* in 1995. She also served as guest curator for an exhibit of Jan Luyken genre drawings and prints at the Amsterdam Historical Museum in 1997.

Dutch-born co-curator **Peter G. Rose** is a food historian, syndicated food columnist, and historical event-planner. She has written articles for, among many others, *Gourmet*, *Saveur*, and the *New York Times*. Her books include *Foods of the Hudson* and *The Sensible Cook: Dutch Foodways in the Old and New World*, which contains a translation of the 1683 edition of *De Verstandige Kock*, the definitive Dutch cookbook of the seventeenth century.

Rose has lectured extensively on Dutch and Dutch American foodways at, among others, the Smithsonian, the Corcoran Gallery of Art, Harvard University's Fogg Museum, Hofstra University, the Culinary Institute of America, and, in the Netherlands, Rotterdam's Museum Boymans-Van Beuningen. She was also a planner and researcher for the exhibit *One Man's Trash is Another Man's Treasure: The Metamorphosis of the European Utensil in the New World* at the Museum Boymans-Van Beuningen, writing an extensive essay for its catalog. She belongs to the Speakers in the Humanities Program of the New York Council for the Humanities.

She organized events and created historically appropriate menus for the Peter Stuyvesant Ball at the Waldorf Astoria, EAB Bank at the New-York Historical Society and the John Carter Brown Library, among many others.

She has appeared on television in a variety of programs, including "Goodday, New York" and the Food Network. Her website can be visited at www.peterrose.com.

CONTENTS

ILLUSTRATIONS

STATEMENT FROM THE MAYOR OF ALBANY

In 2002, the City of Albany marks the 350th anniversary of the founding in 1652 of Beverwijck—the Dutch settlement that has become present-day Albany. This milestone has provided a wonderful opportunity for the city to celebrate its Dutch heritage while simultaneously showcasing its revitalization.

One of the highlights of the city's celebration is the exhibition Matters of Taste: Food and Drink in Seventeenth-Century Dutch Art and Life (September 20–December 8, 2002), accompanied by the publication of this book and related public programs, all organized by the Albany Institute of History & Art.

The Albany Institute is uniquely qualified to serve as the coordinator of and the exclusive venue for Matters of Taste. Founded in 1791, the institute is one of the country's oldest museums, with a nationally recognized collection. It is also the premier cultural institution devoted to the history, art, and culture of Albany and the upper Hudson Valley. The museum's recent $17.8 million construction project has expanded its presence in Albany and demonstrates a high level of service to our community.

The citywide Beverwijck celebration showcases the true spirit of collaboration among local government, arts and cultural organizations, businesses, and community groups. It also fosters important linkages that will help strengthen the city's long-term tourism and economic development efforts.

This book is a permanent record of this wonderful project and will be a lasting memento of both the city's 350th anniversary celebration and the influence of Dutch heritage on Albany and the Hudson Valley.

Gerald D. Jennings
Mayor, City of Albany

COLLECTIONS

Allen Memorial Art Museum, Oberlin College

Isabel and Alfred Bader

Brooklyn Museum of Art

The Detroit Institute of Arts

Teresa Heinz and the late Senator John Heinz

Hofstra Museum, Hofstra University

Lawrence Steigrad Fine Arts

Memorial Art Gallery of the University of Rochester

The Metropolitan Museum of Art

Milwaukee Art Museum

Mr. and Mrs. Harry Judson Moore, Judson Galleries Inc.

Museum of Fine Arts, Boston

The Museum of Fine Arts, Houston

National Gallery of Art, Washington, D.C.

Otto Naumann Ltd., New York

New Orleans Museum of Art

The New-York Historical Society

North Carolina Museum of Art

Peter Tillou Works of Art

Philadelphia Museum of Art

Private Collection

University of Virginia Art Museum

Van Cortlandt House Museum

Wadsworth Atheneum Museum of Art

The Henry H. Weldon Collection

Worcester Art Museum

DIRECTOR'S FOREWORD | MATTERS OF TASTE: FOOD AND DRINK IN SEVENTEENTH-CENTURY DUTCH ART AND LIFE

The Albany Institute is pleased to present the book *Matters of Taste: Food and Drink in Seventeenth-Century Dutch Art and Life* in celebration of the 350th anniversary (1652–2002) of the founding of Beverwijck, the name of the original Dutch settlement now known as Albany.

Shortly after explorer Henry Hudson's voyage to the upper Hudson in 1609, tales of abundant furs and other riches encouraged Dutch traders, under the auspices of the West India Company, to establish a trading post in 1624 near what is now Albany. Although the Dutch controlled this area for fewer than fifty years, there is still a Dutch presence in Albany today.

In light of this history and rich cultural heritage, the Albany Institute is publishing *Matters of Taste* to accompany an exhibition by the same name. The book features sixty seventeenth-century Dutch and Flemish still-life and genre paintings (scenes of daily life) in which food and drink play a dominant role. The paintings document the bounty of land and sea and its presentation during the Netherlands' golden age, when New Netherland was in its infancy.

Drawn exclusively from American museums, art galleries, and private collections, paintings by Dutch masters such as Pieter de Hooch, Jan Steen, Adriaen van Ostade, Jan Davidsz. de Heem, Pieter Claesz., and Gerret Willemsz. Heda portray epicurean delights against backdrops of taverns, open markets, kitchens, and tabletops, in the presence of cooks, scullery maids, brewers, bakers, fishmongers, and pancake makers. They are reminiscent of the paintings owned by New Netherland settlers like Hendrick Kip, a public official who arrived in 1637 with an art collection that included a landscape by Vincent Leckerbetien, or New Amsterdam surgeon and barber Jacob De Lange, whose estate inventory listed six banquet scenes, two still lifes, a genre scene of a cobbler, two rustic views, and a picture of a plucked cock.

This volume begins with an insightful essay by Dr. Charles T. Gehring, director of the New Netherland Project, that sets the stage for the founding of Beverwijck by highlighting the physical, political, and social aspects of the 1652 settlement. Art historian Nancy T. Minty then recounts the history and popularity of collecting seventeenth-century still-life and genre paintings in the United States.

The next essay, by guest curator Donna R. Barnes, a professor of education at Hofstra University, provides a fascinating account of Dutch art as it relates to images of food and drink and the symbolism found in the paintings.

Finally, guest curator Peter G. Rose, a food historian, presents a lively discussion of Dutch and Dutch American culinary history, with insights into ingredients, preparation, and cooking. Included as a special supplement to *Matters of Taste* is a cookbook, *Dutch Recipes with an American Connection*, that features recipes from the 1683 edition of *De Verstandige Kock* (The sensible cook), translated and adapted for today's kitchen by Peter G. Rose.

In the catalog section of this book, Barnes and Rose supplement the feast for the eyes with dual perspectives on each work of art that provide food for thought and a sampling of Dutch foodways. Jointly, they serve up a delicious Dutch treat that focuses on the artistic and culinary traditions of the Netherlands and their impact on New Netherland.

Peter G. Rose's vivid descriptions of the foodstuffs available to the first Dutch settlers are drawn from a number of colonial accounts. Specific references to Beverwijck and Albany abound. In his 1655 *Description of the New Netherlands*, Adriaen van der Donck (c.1620–1655), sheriff of Rensselaerswijck—the Van Rensselaer patroonship, located on the upper Hudson—proclaimed Beverwijck, then a trading outpost, to be "a land of Abundance," with "venison [which] digests easily and is good food [and] the wild turkey large, heavy, fat and fine," adding that rivers teemed with fish, especially pike and sturgeon, and native fruits and vegetables grew in profusion along their banks and in woodlands (1968).

Because the Dutch settlers brought the seeds to New Netherland from Holland, Van der Donck was also able to list the produce in Beverwijck's gardens, where cabbages, parsnips, carrots, beets, endive, succory (chicory), fennel, sorrel, dill, spinach, radishes, parsley, chervil, cresses, onions, and leeks were cultivated for salad, a Dutch specialty introduced into England by Dutch immigrants in the time of Shakespeare. He mentions indigenous crops like pumpkins, and the "three sisters"—squash, corn, and beans—which were raised and traded by Native Americans. *Sapaen* (cornmeal mush), a staple of the Indian diet, was a favorite food in both communities and an example of the colonists' adaptation of New World foods as substitutes for traditional Dutch products unavailable to them.

The Dutch diet emphasized dairy products and bread. Most settlers kept milk cows, like the small herd of five mentioned in the 1648 inventory of the estate of the Widow Bronck of Emaus, in what is now the Bronx. They also cultivated grains like wheat and oats on the arable flood plains of the Hudson River, using them as the chief ingredients in two food staples, beer and bread; by 1650 there were already six or seven bakers and a host of brewers situated in Beverwijck. Hogs, also mentioned in the Widow Bronck's estate inventory as "running [wild] in the woods," were the favorite meat (Bronck 1648).

Charles Wooley, an English chaplain stationed in New York City between 1678 and 1680, noted, "The [Dutch] feast freely at the Funeral of any Friend, [and] eat and drink very plentifully at the Feasts," referring to their consumption of brandy wine, a mixture of brandy and raisins served in *brandewijnkom* (two-handled silver-paneled bowls) that were passed at weddings, funerals, and other rites of passage (Cornell 1968).

In the early 1740s Alexander Hamilton, a Maryland physician, observed in his *Itinerarium*, "the [Albany] Dutch here keep their houses very neat ... and their kitchens are likewise very clean. They hang earthen or delft plates and dishes all round the walls ... [and] set out their cabinets and bouffetts much with china." He refers to their "constant diet of salt provisions in the winter." In the company of the patroon, Jeremias van Rensselaer II (1705–1745), Hamilton also enjoyed "good viands and wine" (Hamilton 1907).

During the mid-eighteenth century, Swedish naturalist Peter Kalm (1716–1779) reported on Albany's persistently Dutch palate, particularly the introduction of tea, coffee, and hot chocolate, which by then were popular in the Netherlands. "Their food and its preparation is very different from the English," Kalm noted. "Breakfast is tea, commonly without milk ... Dinner is buttermilk and bread ... with a large salad, prepared with an abundance of vinegar and very little or no oil. They commonly drink very weak beer or pure water" (1987). He was impressed that thrifty Dutch housewives prepared just enough food for the meal but paid close attention to housecleaning and good cooking, which were considered important traits.

The young Scot Anne Macvicar (later Grant) observed in the late 1760s that Dutch American households in Albany were somewhat anglicized. She noted that "Tea was a perfect regale, being served up with various sorts of cakes ... cold pastry, and great quantities of sweetmeats and preserved fruits of various kinds, and plates of hickory and other nuts ready cracked. In all manner of confectionery and pastry

these people excelled; and having fruit in great plenty, which cost them nothing, and getting sugar home at an easy rate, in return for their exports to the West Indies, the quantity of these articles used in families otherwise plain and frugal was astonishing" (Grant 1809).

On the eve of the American Revolution, in 1771, Abraham Lott, treasurer of the colony, recorded his summer "Voyage to Albany." Although he "drank tea" daily with Dutch Americans like Doctor van Dyke, Lady Westerlo, Colonel van Rensselaer, Mr. Beekman, Mr. Douw, and Mr. Banyar, he also ate meals of "Salad & Parsley, and Milk" at the home of Anthony Ten Eyck, "Bread & Butter, with Soft Eggs and fried Bacon" near East Greenbush, "Snock [sic], that is Pike" at Albany, a "Supper of Milk & Rusks" at Lebanon, and "Venison and Tea with Mrs. Bronck" at the McCartys' in Coeymans (Lott 1870).

By the late eighteenth century the Dutch character of Albany began to fade as immigrants from New England, Ireland, Germany, and Italy moved into upstate New York, bringing their own foods and ethnic traditions with them. During the twentieth century arrivals from Eastern Europe, the Middle East, Africa, South America, the Caribbean, and Asia introduced diverse cuisines to the region. Nevertheless, Dutch traditions persist, especially during holidays such as Saint Nicholas' Day and New Year's, cultural events like Albany's Tulip Festival and Pinksterfest, and exhibitions like Matters of Taste.

In closing I would like to thank the guest curators and the staff of the Albany Institute, particularly Mary Alice Mackay, research curator, for their extraordinary talent and their efforts in bringing this project to fruition in honor of the three hundred fiftieth anniversary of the founding of the City of Albany. This project would not have been possible without His Excellency Boudewijn van Eenennaam, Ambassador of the Netherlands, or the early support of His Excellency Joris Vos, former Ambassador of the Netherlands, the Honorable Bob Hiensch, Consul General of the Netherlands, and the Honorable Gerald Jennings, Mayor of the City of Albany, or the generosity of Matthew Bender IV and Phoebe Powell Bender.

Christine M. Miles, Executive Director
Albany Institute of History & Art

ACKNOWLEDGMENTS

In the years of preparation for this project, Peter G. Rose and Donna R. Barnes came to be known as "the Dutch team." Jointly we thank the following: Consul General Bob Hiensch and the Netherlands Consulate as well as Henry Z. Kol and Frank Ligtvoet for their sustained interest in the project. Our thanks also to Alexandra van Dongen, Charles T. Gehring, Walter Liedtke, Tara Stack, and Arthur Wheelock. We have enjoyed very much working with Christine M. Miles, Tammis K. Groft, Mary Alice Mackay, Marcia H. Moss, and Diane LaVigna Wixted of the Albany Institute.

DRB and PGR

Hofstra University graciously released me from teaching responsibilities to conduct picture research in the United States and Europe and to write this book. Thanks to President Emeritus James M. Shuart, Provost Herman A. Berliner, Deans James R. Johnson and David Christman, and Professor Karen Osterman for their continuing encouragement and support of my "passion" for Dutch art. Thanks also to Cynthia Serafin-Maus, who served as my research assistant.

Research was enhanced by the cooperation of librarians at the Amsterdam Historical Museum, Rijksprentenkabinet in Amsterdam, Rijksbureau voor Kunsthistorische Documentatie in The Hague, the Thomas J. Watson Library at the Metropolitan Museum of Art, the New York Public Library, the Frick Art Reference Library, and the Axinn Library of Hofstra University.

For several years, the Amsterdam Historical Museum has welcomed this "visiting scholar" by providing working space and collegial enthusiasm for this and other Dutch art projects. The generosity of its director, Pauline Kruseman, and her colleagues is deeply appreciated.

Many individuals graciously provided assistance: Candace Adelson, Isabel and Alfred Bader, Ronni Baer, Cees Bakker, Petra van den Born, Chris de Bruijn, Cara Dennison, Marjorie Easton, Michael Enthoven, Gail Feigenbaum, Suzanne Foley, Margaret Glover, Jennifer Ickes, Michiel Jonker, George Keyes, Jack Kilgore, Zeljko Latković, Katherine Luber, Corry Massingh-van der Wielen, Harry Judson Moore, Otto Naumann, Nancy Norwood, Michiel Plomp, Patricia Phagen, Joseph Rishel, William Robinson, Sam Segal, Kevin Stayton, Lawrence Steigrad, Peter Sutton, Peter Tillou, Roberta Waddell, George Way, Henry and June Weldon, Dennis Weller, James Welu, and Laurie Winters.

Barbara Miller, as always, offered her continuing support and encouragement with patience, tact, and good humor; without her help it would have been impossible to complete this engaging enterprise. Her untimely death in January 2002 has made it impossible for her to see the fruits of this project, but her spirit hovers over the pages.

Donna R. Barnes, Ed. D., Hofstra University

Over the years, Dutch food historian Joop Witteveen has been invariably gracious and immensely helpful. I am deeply grateful to him. My heartfelt appreciation also goes to American food historian Stephen Schmidt, who allowed me to benefit from his experience. In addition, I would like to express my gratitude to the following: Johannes van Dam, Charles Danowski, Christine Danowski, Marie Louise Donarski, John de Jong, Peter de Jong, Joe DiMauro, Dennis Maika, Marleen van der Molen, Jerry Novesky, and Marietje van Winter.

I am most sincerely grateful to my best friend and husband, Don, for his constant help, reassurance, and encouragement. Without him none of this would be possible. Our wonderful daughter, Peter Pamela, continues to enchant us with her love, talent, and generosity.

Peter G. Rose, Food Historian

Matters of Taste: Food and Drink in Seventeenth-Century Dutch Art and Life

THE FOUNDING OF BEVERWIJCK, 1652

THE MORNING sun glistened across the broad river, illuminating the Dutch village on the far shore, as the cycle of daily life began. Milk cows, released from their stalls at the rear of the houses, made their way to the area around the church. After counting his wards for the day, the herdsman marched them down the road to the common pasture near the fort. At about the same time three blasts of a horn signaled that one of the many bakeries was open for business. This scene could have occurred in any one of a thousand Dutch villages along the Rhine or Maas. However, the mountains in the distance and the presence of Native Americans everywhere indicated a setting in the New World.

The Dutch community lay on the upper Hudson River, in New Netherland, at a strategic location dominating the North American fur trade for the West India Company. After the construction of Fort Orange in 1624 a settlement began to develop near the fort, both for protection and for proximity to the fur trade. The Dutch had developed a vigorous trade shortly after Henry Hudson's arrival in the area aboard the *Halve Maen* in 1609, exchanging *sewant* or *wampum* produced by Native Americans along the Connecticut shore for furs brought down the Mohawk Valley by Iroquois traders. Almost by accident the West India Company had gained control of the only known passage to the interior of North America south of the Saint Lawrence River.

As they gathered to exploit their geographic advantage near the confluence of the Mohawk and Hudson Rivers, the Dutch, like every group of settlers, brought their own culture and customs and created a community in the image of their homeland. With each group of settlers came the cultural traits and attributes of the homeland. These cultural roots were planted so deeply that well into the nineteenth century, long after the English takeover of New Netherland in 1664, visitors to what became the Albany area were struck by the persistent Dutch influence there. Although many early settlers came from other countries in Europe, they soon adopted the Dutch language and began the long process of acculturation.

Because of the settlement's isolated location 120 miles north of Manhattan Island, the first settlers were forced to become self-reliant. When the river froze during the winter months boat traffic ceased until the ice broke in the spring. Not only did the inhabitants have to survive harsh winters without prospect of outside relief but they were also surrounded by potential enemies: the French in Canada to the north, the English in New England to the east, the so-called River Indians to the south, and the Iroquois to the west. It was not an enviable situation, but the fur trade—the core of New Netherland's economy—depended on the survival of this fragile Dutch settlement on the northern frontier.

In spite of the dangers surrounding them, the Dutch settlers were up to the task. With them came all the various trades necessary for survival in an isolated and remote location. There were carpenters, wheelwrights, coopers, blacksmiths, brickmakers, and, most important of all, people skilled in baking bread and brewing beer—the two major components of the daily diet in the seventeenth century. Fortunately, the rich soil along the Hudson was able to produce the grain and hops necessary to accommodate both trades.

By the time the expanding community around Fort Orange was given a local government under the name of Beverwijck, a growing number of bakeries and breweries were already serving the population. The court of Fort Orange and Dorp Beverwijck was carved out of the heart of Rensselaerswijck—a patroonship owned by the powerful Van Rensselaer family that had been in a jurisdictional dispute with Petrus Stuyvesant, the director general of New Netherland. Rensselaerswijck claimed that because the West India Company's fort and trading post lay in the middle of its territory even the land under the fort belonged to the patroon. Stuyvesant countered that not only did the land under the fort belong to the West India Company but so did a "field of fire" around the fort. He reasoned that as the only fortified protection in the area the integrity of the fort had to be maintained. However, reason did not prevail. After four years of contention between the two parties, Stuyvesant resolved the issue in the spring of 1652, by proclaiming that all the land falling within a three-thousand-foot arc around the fort was henceforth under the jurisdiction of the West India Company. *Matters of Taste: Food and Drink in Seventeenth-Century Dutch Art and Life* is presented in 2002 to celebrate the 350th anniversary of the founding of Beverwijck.

Overnight many of the inhabitants of Rensselaerswijck abjured their oaths to the patroon and chose to swear allegiance to the West India Company. Unfortunately for the patroonship, most of the craftsmen and tradesmen, including the majority of the brewers and bakers, fell within the three-thousand-foot arc. This new local jurisdiction also included other settlements south of the patroonship, such as the Esopus [Kingston], which did not receive a separate court until 1661. The governing body of Beverwijck was called a *kleine banck van justitie* (an inferior bench of judicature), which performed executive, legislative, and judicial functions for the community. Among the actions taken by this body, which met every Tuesday in a regular session, were ordinances reflecting local needs and issues.

Many of the locally drafted ordinances concerned the sale of baked goods to the Native American population. During the summer months the village was flooded with Indians loaded with packs of furs. The prospect of acquiring furs—almost the equivalent of gold— drove the inhabitants to resort to various means to negotiate with the Indians. One way was to entice them with various baked goods. Such actions prompted the court of Fort Orange and Beverwijck to pass ordinances directed specifically to this issue, notably a prohibition against baking bread with sugar, currants, raisins, or prunes, and another prohibition against baking only during the summer months. It also passed ordinances intended to discourage unscrupulous traders by banning their use of alcohol to gain an advantage in negotiations.

The Dutch village of Beverwijck managed to survive in its precarious location by adhering to the principles of political and social institutions transmitted from the Netherlands and adapting to an environment different in many ways from the homeland. The people were as flexible as they were hardy, and as culturally diverse as the population of Amsterdam, the city responsible for New Netherland's well-being within the structure of the West India Company.

Although the fur trade gradually declined in importance, it was replaced by other industries that exploited the natural resources of the region, such as lumber, grain, and clay. The streams draining into the Hudson supplied water power for numerous saw- and gristmills while the presence of large amounts of high-quality clay along the banks of the Hudson provided the raw material for the production of bricks and pantiles—enough to export as far away as Fort Casimir (New Castle, Delaware) on the Delaware River. However, Beverwijck's major asset remained its location. Long after Beverwijck was renamed Albany in 1664, the confluence of the Mohawk and the Hudson Rivers remained the only passageway to the west below Canada. It was only a matter of time before a canal was constructed to open the interior of the country, turning Albany into a commercial crossroads and New York City into an international cultural and economic center.

Charles T. Gehring
Director, New Netherland Project

A MOVEABLE FEAST: THE AMERICAN APPETITE FOR NETHERLANDISH GENRE AND STILL-LIFE PAINTINGS

SINCE the early 1800s, when collections of old master works were first recorded in this country, Americans have demonstrated and sustained a particular taste for Dutch and Flemish genre and still-life paintings. The selection presented here features sixty Netherlandish still-life, domestic, and "low-life" paintings, and it celebrates the historic interest in these subjects from 1871 through the present. The initial year signifies the date of the Metropolitan Museum of Art's seminal purchase of more than 150 Dutch and Flemish old masters, including both *Still Life with Oysters* by Jan Davidsz. de Heem (1606–c. 1683) and *The Newborn Baby* by Matthijs Naiveu (1647–1726) (see cats. 24 and 33). Other selections reflect later American tastes, which have developed to incorporate the rarefied aesthetic of artists like Adriaen Coorte (c. 1660–after 1723) and Harmen van Steenwijck (1612–c. 1655 or later) (see cats. 20, 21, 53, 54, and 55).

The narrative told by these paintings touches on some of the country's most influential early collectors, such as Detroit's Mr. and Mrs. James E. Scripps (1835–c. 1906), and Philadelphia's John Graver Johnson (1841–1917), as well as their latter-day successors, notably Henry H. Weldon, Michael Enthoven, the late Senator John Heinz (1938–1991), Alfred Bader, and his friend Harry Judson Moore. It also incorporates the names of two art historians critical to the appreciation of Dutch and Flemish painting in America, Wilhelm R. Valentiner (1880–1958) and Wolfgang Stechow (1896–1974).

The sheer viewing pleasure offered by these generally small and finely crafted "cabinet" paintings suffices to explain their appeal. Nonetheless, for nineteenth-century Americans the aesthetic enticement of such paintings was at least equaled, if not surpassed, by a perceived morality. In the words of Alfred Trumble (c. 1844–1897), editor of the art magazine *The Collector*, the reputed integrity of a national character pervaded its school of painters: "Serious, solid, sincere—Dutch national characteristics—the characteristics of Dutch art" (1899). Since Americans viewed the Dutch as sensible, sober, and simple, their paintings were in turn interpreted in that clean, clear light; hence, the tremendous resonance and reassurance in scenes of quiet domesticity and labor.

The painter most prized by American collectors for his evocations of domestic quietude was Pieter de Hooch (1629–1684). Early critic Charles H. Caffin (1854–1918), speaking for the American sensibility and acknowledging de Hooch's proficiency in 1909, proclaimed that his paintings were "veritable poems of light, wrought with extraordinary conscientiousness and to a high pitch of refinement" (Caffin 1909, 121–22). Moreover, when Caffin elaborated on the artist, he echoed the familiar and popular theme of the scrupulousness of Dutch society and its painters: "[N]o artist has been so successful in rendering what visitors to Holland rarely fail to observe—the propriety and cleanliness of the Dutch home, and the sentiment that seems to attach to every object in it and around it."

De Hooch's enduring appeal was confirmed in the 1998-1999 exhibition of his paintings, many drawn from American holdings, organized by Peter Sutton at the Wadsworth Atheneum in Hartford, Connecticut, and the Dulwich Picture Gallery, England. De Hooch is represented here by *The Fireside* (*Woman and a Serving Woman at a Hearth*) (see cat. 27) from the North Carolina Museum of Art, where it was acquired under the eye of Wilhelm Valentiner in 1952. The German-born Valentiner first came to America in the early 1900s to work at the Metropolitan Museum of Art, where, in 1909, he staged the "Hudson-Fulton Exhibition," which included about 150 Dutch old masters from American collections. He went on to advise a number of important American collectors and to become director of both the Detroit Institute of Arts and the North Carolina Museum of Art. Interestingly, *The Fireside* (*Woman and a Serving Woman at a Hearth*) had previously belonged to the Chicago lumber heir Martin A. Ryerson, who was both a benefactor and director of the Art Institute of Chicago.

Quiringh Gerritsz. van Brekelenkam (c. 1620–c. 1668), represented here by three interiors featuring household and motherly duties as well as one vegetable vendor (see cats. 15, 16, 17, and 18), also featured prominently in nineteenth-century American inventories. In fact the market scene exhibited here (see cat. 18) belonged to the Detroit newspaper publisher James E. Scripps, who in 1889 gave the painting along with about eighty others, mostly by Dutch and Italian old masters, to the Detroit Institute of Arts (then known as the Detroit Museum of Art). A later American acquisition of Van Brekelenkam's work, the *Mother and Child in an Interior* (see cat. 17), was presented in 1972 to the Allen Memorial Art Museum at Oberlin College, Ohio, in honor of Wolfgang Stechow. The German-born Stechow's long affiliation with Oberlin and its museum marked a distinguished art historical career, which influenced many collectors and institutions in the United States.

In spite of the considerable number of representations of Netherlandish virtue in nineteenth-century American collections, both private and public, the country's apparent taste for high-minded and upstanding subjects was belied by the significant presence of "low-life" scenes featuring such subjects as tavern interiors, with drinking, brawling, gaming, and smoking. In the United States the favorite practitioners of this genre have traditionally been the Flemish painters David Teniers II (1610–1690) and Adriaen Brouwer (c. 1605–1638), along with their Dutch contemporaries Jan Steen (1626–1679) and Adriaen van Ostade (1610–1685). Again and again, our nineteenth-century critics were at pains to reconcile the evident weakness of Americans for distasteful subject matter to the allegedly edifying properties of fine art. Like their French and English predecessors, our theorists and tastemakers fixed on the immaculate brushwork of the bawdy scenes as their redeeming virtue. Descriptions of northern European works are redolent with terminology that suggests a morality of technique, associated with our idealized view of the Dutch national character. When the author and critic Henry James reviewed the inaugural exhibition at the Metropolitan Museum of Art in 1871, which was dominated by Netherlandish baroque paintings, he lauded the straightforward honesty of the Dutch school: "We know what it is to have turned with a sort of moral relief, in the galleries of Italy, to some stray specimen of Dutch patience and conscience" (James 1872).

A similar note is struck in the words of John Graver Johnson, the first American to fix on Jan Steen, purchasing at least twelve works attributed to his hand, when he claimed that the artist combined: "coarseness of subject with refinement of execution" (Johnson 1892, 26). (Johnson is notable in American collecting history not just for his prescient taste in Steen but chiefly for amassing more than one thousand old master paintings which he bequeathed to Philadelphia and which now belong to the Philadelphia Museum of Art.) While Steen's *Prayer Before the Meal*, one of Johnson's outstanding choices (see cat. 52), is ostensibly pious, it is also subversive and suggestive. Many of the other Steens acquired by him, like those in numerous American collections (for example, the *Twelfth Night* [see cat. 51] purchased by Boston's Museum of Fine Arts in 1954), were even more overtly raucous. Steen's enduring popularity in this country is confirmed by the 1996–1997 exhibition of his work organized by the National Gallery of Art in Washington, D.C. and the Rijksmuseum, Amsterdam.

Likewise, Adriaen van Ostade was and still is admired by American enthusiasts of the "low-life" genre. His work is represented here by a characteristic peasant scene from the Brooklyn Museum of Art (see cat. 38).

Once again, Charles Caffin, writing on Ostade, noted the disparity between his undignified subjects and refined technique: "The figures are squat and lumpish, curiously like animated roly-poly puddings, only redeemed from commonness by the limpid coloring and the suave, facile manner of the brushwork" (Caffin 1909, 109).

The dichotomy of a smooth, immaculate technique softening a rough subject culminates in the shimmering, silken brothel interiors of the Dutch painters, typified here by *Scene in a Bordello* (see cat. 42), by Hendrick Pot (c. 1585–1657). This painting is now in the New Orleans Museum of Art, a gift from the collector Bert Piso. While earlier American inventories did include such paintings, they tended to obscure the suggestive subject matter with euphemistic titles like "Merriment" or "Revelry."

Historically, the genre of still life has inspired the highest technical refinement in its practitioners. In spite of its lowly theoretical status (always ranked below history painting and portraiture), still-life painting has elicited rhapsodic responses. Seventeenth-century Netherlandish painters prided themselves on their mastery of illusionist technique, and it is this aspect of their work that has consistently transfixed American collectors steeped in the nineteenth-century aesthetic of materialism, truth, naturalism, and realism. Dutch and Flemish still lifes have always been coveted in this country, except, notably, by such Gilded Age masterpiece collectors as Peter Arrell Brown Widener (1834–1915) of Philadelphia, Henry Clay Frick (1849–1919) and Benjamin Altman (1840–1913) of New York, and Andrew Mellon (1855–1937) of Washington, D.C., who targeted large, impressive canvases by the biggest names.

Willem Kalf (1619–1693) was and remains one of the Dutch still-life painters most prized by American collectors. His work is represented here by a copy from the New York Gallery of Fine Arts Collection amassed by Luman Reed (1789–1836)—now at the New-York Historical Society—and an autograph painting lent by collector Peter Tillou of New York (see cats. 28 and 29). Likewise Jan Davidsz. de Heem has endured in the American eye from 1871, when the Metropolitan Museum of Art bought his diminutive *Still Life with a Glass and Oysters*, through the Rochester Memorial Art Gallery's purchase in 1949 of his more elaborate *Still Life* (see cats. 24 and 25) and beyond. Both of these paintings perfectly exemplify the power and appeal of illusion.

Abraham van Beyeren (c. 1620–1690), a third Dutch still-life painter beloved by Americans, is featured in grander, more elaborate works: the lavish fruit piece lent by a private collector and *Preparations for a Meal*, a painting from the Detroit Institute of Arts acquired by Valentiner (see cats. 5 and 6). Pieter Claesz. (c. 1597–c. 1661) also belongs to the group of still-life painters traditionally favored in this country. He is represented here by an intimate table-top composition lent by Alfred Bader, who usually collects biblical subjects but could not resist such a discovery in rural England in the mid-1950s (see cat. 19).

In recent decades the American appreciation of the still-life genre has increased in scope and sophistication, admitting new names to the canon. One such is Adriaen Coorte, little known until the Dutch scholar Laurens Bol rediscovered him in the late 1950s. His tantalizing yet simple *Wild Strawberries on a Ledge* and *Chestnuts on a Ledge* (see cats. 20 and 21), lent by Henry H. Weldon, are treasured by that collector as small marvels. Likewise, the identity of Clara Peeters (1594–c. 1640), the only female painter shown here, who was active from about 1607 until after 1621, was subsumed by archival confusion until quite recently. A glistening example from her brush is her *Still Life with Crab, Shrimps, and Lobster* from the Museum of Fine Arts, Houston, a gift of Michael Enthoven (see cat. 40).

A third painter, the enigmatic Harmen van Steenwijck, was virtually unknown in this country until the later twentieth century. His work is featured here in two paintings from the Heinz Family collection: highly stylized and refined laden tables, subject matter befitting a family famous for its food products (see cats. 53 and 54). The Heinz collection is the most extensive private American holding of northern European still lifes, numbering about seventy works. Van Steenwijck is also represented by a fruit and game piece belonging to a private collector (see cat. 55), a transplanted Dutchman who began his collection of Dutch and Flemish paintings with still lifes at a time when illness precluded indulging in the pleasures of the table and feasting was restricted to the eye and the mind.

As Americans continue to free themselves from traditional prejudices regarding the strict hierarchy of genres, with history painting and portraiture rated far above "low-life" and still-life subjects, and as they become more imaginative and inclusive in their acceptance of rediscovered names, collectors and the viewing public may look forward to enriched holdings and an even fatter feast for the eyes.

Nancy T. Minty
Art Historian

DUTCH PAINTINGS IN THE SEVENTEENTH CENTURY

UNDERSTANDING THE HISTORICAL CONTEXT

IN THE seventeenth century, the seven United Provinces of the Dutch Republic consisted of Holland (the most politically and economically prominent and most heavily populated), Utrecht, Gelderland, Friesland, Groningen, Overijssel, and Zeeland. These provinces were essentially Protestant and enjoyed considerable prosperity. Both factors contributed to the production of paintings and other works of graphic, architectural, literary, and decorative art in a time now known as the Dutch Golden Age.

The northern Netherlands became Protestant when the Reformation swept over Northern Europe during the sixteenth century, while the southern Netherlands (consisting of the provinces of Brabant, Limburg, and Flanders), still under Spanish control, remained Roman Catholic. The Dutch were attracted to Calvinism, although different Protestant denominations found adherents to the dismay of both Catholic and Protestant absolute monarchies elsewhere in Europe. Spain committed atrocities against Netherlanders in the sixteenth century following a stormy period of Protestant iconoclasm beginning in 1566, during which Catholic churches, monasteries, and convents were looted, vandalized, and destroyed. This iconoclasm marked the beginning of the Dutch Reformation; remaining Catholic properties were confiscated for Protestant or municipal use.

Calvinism became the country's official religion with the Synods of Dordrecht in 1618 and 1622. However, Roman Catholics continued to live in the Netherlands, worshipping privately, often in *schuilkerken* (hidden churches) that were tolerated by city dwellers even as they were decried from Protestant pulpits. Sephardic Jews, escaping the Inquisition in Spain and Portugal, and Ashkenazi Jews, escaping pogroms in central Europe, found a safe haven to live, work, and worship in the Dutch Republic.

Unlike Roman Catholics, Protestants objected to depictions of the saints and biblical scenes as idolatrous and whitewashed their church walls instead, leaving them largely unadorned. That meant that Dutch painters were not commissioned to provide ornamentation for places of Protestant worship and residences of ecclesiastics, nor for private devotional art, as they had before the Reformation. The Protestants removed images of both New and Old Testament figures from churches, believing they interfered with the new ritual.

As a result, the market for religious art declined dramatically. Yet biblical scenes, especially events from the Old Testament and the Apocrypha, were purchased by the educated Dutch citizenry, who used them to adorn their homes but not their houses of worship.

Some early sixteenth-century Dutch and Flemish artists chose to set religious images amidst more secular imagery and themes. Pieter Aertsen (c. 1507 – 1575) and his pupil, Joachim Beuckelaer (c. 1533 – c. 1575), pioneered in the depiction of kitchen and market scenes with scriptural images of "The Flight into Egypt," "Jesus in the House of Martha and Mary," "The

Supper at Emmaus," "Lazarus in the House of the Rich Man," or "Christ and the Woman Taken in Adultery." By the seventeenth century, however, painters were less likely to include these religious subjects in secularized market scenes (see cats. 1, 8, 18, 44, and 59).

PROSPERITY PRODUCES NEW CLIENTS FOR ART

In spite of a paucity of natural resources, the industrious Dutch created a flourishing capitalist economy based heavily on fishing, manufacturing, and trade. Dutch ships, owned and operated by the East and West India Companies, traveled to the far corners of the globe. Private vessels, often jointly owned, traded with European partners. Fishing sloops and herring busses trawled the North Sea. Whalers traveled to the Arctic regions. Sailboats and cargo and passenger barges plied the inland waterways connecting most cities.

Investment in trade and banking generated wealth. Dutch butter and cheese, preserved herring and salted cod, textiles and manufactured items were exchanged for goods as diverse as furs, leather, tobacco, wine, olive oil, lumber, porcelain, paper, silk, salt, copper, iron and steel, spices, sugar (and later tea and coffee), human slaves, and, most fundamentally, the cereal grains known collectively as the "Mother Trade"—wheat, rye, oats, and barley. These grains were imported for use in the Netherlands' all-important baking and brewing industries.

An influx of immigrants from Flanders, France, England, Central Europe, and Scandinavia provided a substantial work force, ranging from dock workers and sailors to skilled weavers and diamond cutters, artists, merchants, physicians, surgeons, scientists, theologians, and university professors, most escaping from persecution or penury elsewhere. All played a part in building and strengthening the Dutch economy. The population tripled between 1550 and 1650, rapidly swelling the cities of Amsterdam, Rotterdam, Haarlem, Leiden, The Hague, Delft, Dordrecht, Alkmaar, Enkhuizen, and Hoorn in the province of Holland.

Prosperity persisted despite the Eighty Years' War with Spain, which began in 1568 and ended in 1648 with recognition of the hard-won independence of the Netherlands in the Treaty of Westphalia. Frequent Anglo-Dutch hostilities also occurred, including three wars at sea during the 1650s, 1660s, and early 1670s. France invaded the Netherlands in 1672, during the Rampjaar, or "disaster year." Although these wars caused some hardships, they were also good for certain businesses, especially shipbuilding and cannon foundries. The Trip brothers, who sold tar for ships and munitions, and the De Geers, who profited handsomely and made fortunes in spite of wartime, were noted patrons of the arts.

Over the seventeenth century, the Dutch became the most literate people in Europe. Amsterdam, the center of world trade, became the center of European book publishing, where the trade in ideas complemented the trade in goods. Books were printed in more than twenty different languages. Subjects ranged from religion to poetry, fiction, travel accounts, Latin and Greek classics, self-help or "how-to" manuals, treatises on medicine, anatomy, and pharmacy, and emblem books. The Dutch also published maps, pamphlets, broadsheets, songbooks, and newspapers, many illustrated with etchings and engravings.

Emblem books—notably works by Roemer Visscher, Jacob Cats, Adriaen van de Venne, and Jan Luyken—combined images with rhymed texts, learned quotations, or biblical verses to invite contemplation of moral or religious ideas.

Books of advice, sought by wealthy merchant-class owners of country houses, formed another rising genre, stimulated by Marcus Doornick's 1668 publication in Amsterdam of Jan van der Groen's *Den Nederlantsen Hovenier* (The Dutch gardener). Van der Groen, former gardener to the Prince of Orange, included tips on gardening and landscaping in his book; descriptions of vegetables, herbs, and fruits and their uses; and designs for ornamental latticework, fountains, and cold frames. The volume was later extended and bound with other treatises into *Het Vermakelijck Landtleven* (The pleasurable country life), which also included the anonymously written *De Verstandige Kock* (The sensible cook) with its two appendixes—"De Hollantse Slacht-tijdt" (The Dutch butchering time) and "De Verstandige Confituur-maker" (The sensible confectioner). (See Peter Rose's essay, "Dutch Foodways: An American Connection.")

The Dutch had a rich cornucopia of foods and spices available, and during the seventeenth century were the best-fed population in Europe. Imported foods included French, German, Italian, and Spanish wines; German beer; Prussian and Polish grains; raisins, dates, figs, and nuts from the Mediterranean; sugar from the Caribbean; and spices from India and the Spice Islands. Their own lands and waters served up an abundant supply of fish and shellfish, a plentiful yield of butter and cheese, and the produce of market gardens and orchards made fruitful through recent horticultural innovations and the use of fertilization.

A GROWING MARKET FOR ART

On the demand side of the equation, members of the burgher or merchant class and the aristocracy had money to spend on luxury goods in the seventeenth century—and spend they did. It was their consumerism that contributed to an abundance of visual art during the Golden Age.

Taverns, inns, shops, offices, and even some brothels were decorated with paintings. The greatest demand, however, was for domestic decor. Dutch people enjoyed hanging pictures in their homes.

Municipal institutions, along with the palaces and castles of the nobility, were ornamented with sculptured facades and used sculpture and paintings as interior decoration. The most ambitious example was Amsterdam's New City Hall, begun in 1648. Local leaders of industry, *schutterijen* (local militia groups), medical doctors, and regents and regentesses (directors of municipal charitable institutions) were frequently immortalized in group portraits that adorned guildhalls, *doelen* (practice ranges for guns and crossbows), anatomy theaters, old age homes, orphanages, hospitals, and poor houses.

Schutter portraits often depicted the officers of the guard at banquets, where food was copious and drink flowed freely. Occasionally, the recipients of public charity were also used as subjects, such as a painting by Jan Victors (1620–1676 or after) of orphan girls at mealtime in Amsterdam and another by Werner van den Valckert (c. 1585–c. 1627) of destitute men, women, and children receiving bread.

Dutch paintings traveled across Europe. Pictures were sold to wealthy collectors abroad or given as gifts to foreign rulers, noblemen, and ambassadors. Czar Peter the Great of Russia, after visiting Amsterdam in 1697, brought paintings back to decorate his palace at Peterhof. Early Dutch settlers brought pictures to New Netherland.

On the supply side, there was a plentitude of visual art produced in the Netherlands during the seventeenth century; in fact, some Dutch communities had more artists than butchers. Dutch and Flemish artists occasionally traveled to France and Italy for further training after completing an apprenticeship with a master artist in Holland or Flanders; hence the Italianate influence seen in some Dutch and Flemish pictures (see cat. 58).

Most artists belonged to local guilds, frequently named for St. Luke (since medieval times the patron saint of artists). Guilds often included painters, etchers, engravers, sculptors, architects, art dealers, book publishers, and printers, and, in some communities, tile decorators, faience workers (potters), and glaziers.

The guilds regulated the conditions of apprenticeship; helped to set prices for work; often controlled the sale of an artist's work; and adjudicated disputes among artists, apprentices, and customers. Guilds also served as mutual benefit societies, burying deceased members and occasionally providing financial aid to needy members or their widows. Hundreds of artists worked in the Netherlands during the seventeenth century, producing thousands of paintings, prints, and drawings. Many artists became specialists, renowned for a particular kind of subject matter.

FOOD AND DRINK IN ART

While some patrons favored domestic landscapes, foreign scenes, Dutch cityscapes, or marine pictures featuring Dutch ships and fishing boats, others preferred scenes of daily life (now known as genre paintings). These often depicted taverns, kitchens, open-air markets, or food shops, or festive occasions such as wedding feasts, holiday celebrations, or nursery visits to a mother and her newborn baby. Images of food and drink were frequently included in these scenes.

Food and drink were also the subject matter of *stilleven* (still-life paintings), in which Dutch and Flemish artists excelled. Indeed, the Dutch coined the term. Still-life pictures were frequently classified by their contents. *Ontbijtje* (little breakfast) pictures depicted relatively simple foodstuffs—a herring, ham, or cheese with a bread roll and simple glass of wine or beer—in contrast to the *pronk* (ornately luxurious, even showy or ostentatious) still life known as a *banketje* (little banquet), which displayed more elaborate arrangements of expensive fruits, lobsters and oysters, decorated pies in raised crusts, sumptuous Venetian-style glasses, and serving pieces made of precious metals.

The *tabakje* (little tobacco) was a still life featuring tobacco pipes, smoldering hemp wicks, and *zwavelstokjen* (wooden splinters with sulfur used to light pipes), braziers of burning coals, and jugs of beer or glasses of wine. Not surprisingly, a display of fruit, lavishly arrayed on a silver *tazza* (a shallow, wide-mouthed, footed drinking goblet or compote dish) or more simply placed in a wicker basket, was often designated as a *fruytje* (little fruit). Similarly a still life with a ham prominently displayed (see cats. 10 and 23) was affectionately identified as a *hammetje* (little ham) no matter how large or small the ham.

Some of the wealthiest patrons commissioned portraits—wedding portraits, individual portraits of adults or children, or family portraits that often included household servants and, occasionally, deceased offspring. Food items appeared in family pictures if people were gathered around the dining table. Children were sometimes depicted with fruits, symbolizing the fertile marriages that produced them (see cat. 14).

Less frequently known are portraits of adults with food or drink, although Frans Hals (c. 1582–1666) portrayed a man holding a herring in his *Portrait of Pieter Cornelisz. van der Morsch*. Hals also painted a mad woman, *Malle Babbe*, holding a large pewter drink jug in her hand with a small, knowing owl perched on her shoulder. Other examples include Constantijn Verhout's *Portrait of Cornelisz. Graswinckel(?), the Delft Brewer* with his jug of beer in hand (see cat. 57); Hendrick Bloemaert's portrait-like study, *The Apple Seller* (see cat. 8); and Job Berckheyde's *The Baker* (see cat. 3).

Amusing, often slightly grotesque, portrait-like character studies of adults' heads and faces, frequently utilizing rural peasants, city street characters, or beggars as models, were also popular. Whether used in a painting, print, or drawing, such an image was known as a *tronie*. The identity of the sitter was not particularly important to the image's owner. Occasionally these genrefied portraits depicted tipsy drinkers (see cat. 38), smokers, or gluttons eating.

People also purchased pictures on the open market: at artists' studios; from art dealers or bookshops; in temporary stands at a *kermis* (street fair or carnival); or at public auctions. Some won pictures at lotteries, often organized by artists. Most of these paintings were fairly small in size, suitable for hanging in homes. While some pictures by renowned artists fetched high prices, many were relatively inexpensive, making them available to working-class tailors as well as wealthy upper-class patrons. The Dutch hunger for paintings impressed many foreign visitors. The Englishman William Aglionby, a fellow of the Royal Society, commented that "pictures are very common here [the United Provinces], there being scarce an ordinary tradesman whose house is not decorated with them" (1669).

Estate inventories sometimes indicated the contemporary cash value of pictures as set by a court-appointed appraiser, often another artist. One such case concerned the appraisal in 1680 of the Van der Meulen collection in Amsterdam by Job Berckheyde, then living and working in Haarlem. Judging from these inventories, which itemized the possessions of the deceased room by room, there was no particular pattern for displaying pictures in homes, although some wealthy owners tended to hang still lifes of food or market scenes near the dining area.

Most artists worked alone. However, it was not uncommon for some (even the most prominent) to collaborate on a still-life picture, using one another's special talents in portraying certain elements. Roelof Koets, for example, painted the grapes and vines in a collaboration with Pieter Claesz., who painted the wine glasses, roll, and silver plate (see cat. 31). Another example of a collaborative work features a seascape background by Adam Willaerts with a foreground of fish heaped on the beach by Willem Ormea (see cat. 37).

When artists took on apprentices or students, they often let them work on their paintings, the masters adding the finishing touches and sometimes their signature; this was the case with many "Rembrandt" pictures now attributed to his pupils. Sometimes a master did not sign the work; this seems to have been the case for the *Still Life of Fruit, Oysters, and a Delftware Ewer* produced by Jan Davidsz. de Heem and his workshop (see cat. 26).

Artists were known to repeat themes and visual elements in their works. For example, Pieter Claesz. often used an image of a pewter plate projecting over a table (see cat. 19), while Clara Peeters featured a butter dish in several paintings (see cat. 40). Jan Steen is known to have worked the Twelfth Night celebration (see cat. 51) into at least eight pictures; he borrowed the idea from the Flemish painter Jacob Jordaens (1593–1678).

Artists freely borrowed from and also copied each other's work. Joris van Son reproduced, fish by fish and nearly water droplet by water droplet, a fish still life in a harbor setting first painted by Jan van Kessel the Elder.

Dutch still-life representations of food and drink were prized for many reasons. Some patrons purchased paintings of costly foodstuffs and tableware they were unlikely to own, affording them a certain snob appeal that might impress visitors. This seems particularly true of game pieces, which implied that the owner was of a high social status since hunting was then the privilege of the nobility. Lobsters, not indigenous to much of the Dutch coast, rarely came to market in Holland, so paintings of this cooked crustacean, with its brilliant vermilion colors, implied that the owner knew and valued the finest delicacies. Surely if the palaces of the *stadhouder* (political steward) in Holland were decorated with cornucopia and still lifes, a wine merchant in Dordrecht could follow suit.

The pictures might also have served as "moral compasses"— objects of contemplation and reflection, where the imagery of food and drink reminded the viewer of life's brevity and transitory sensory pleasures, or provided admonitions against luxury, gluttony, drunkenness, or other sinful activities.

Conversely, others may have cherished these images of Holland's bounty and prosperity. Since laughter had to be a frequent response to many genre scenes, many owners might have enjoyed pictures capturing the foibles of peasants and others who behaved boorishly. Likewise, the homely virtues of everyday foods, such as pancakes, prepared lovingly by women discharging their domestic responsibilities, may have provided pleasure for Dutch families.

The Dutch have always enjoyed well-equipped, neat, and orderly clean kitchens with gleaming metal pots and pans scrubbed and scoured to a fare-thee-well, so pictures of these subjects would provide great satisfaction. Finally, true connoisseurs were probably ravished by the painters' artistry, indulging in the visual delight offered by sumptuous images of delicious raw and cooked foods.

Why did Dutch artists paint still-life images of food and drink, or portraits of people with fruits or drinking utensils, or images of people surrounded by food and drink in taverns, markets, kitchens, and scenes of festive occasions? The simplest answer is probably best: there was a market for these images! Painters could earn a living through their artistry. Although few became as wealthy as Jan Davidsz. de Heem, most could support themselves with their brushwork.

TODAY'S VIEWERS

In asking what the pictures now "say" or "mean," present-day art historians have provided a wide range of possible interpretations for the imagery of Dutch and Flemish painters. Many have been influenced by arguments developed by Professors J. A. Emmens and Eddy de Jongh at the University of Utrecht's Art History Institute, who looked for interpretive keys to a better understanding of the imagery by studying literary sources, especially emblem books and contemporary aphorisms and folk-sayings.

From their point of view, there is often far more going on in a seventeenth-century picture than meets the modern eye. Sam Segal, a Dutch scholar who has written extensively on luxury and flower still-life paintings in *A Prosperous Past*, has vigorously argued that point of view for Dutch and Flemish pictures; Peter Sutton, an American art historian, has stated the position eloquently for genre pictures in *Masters of Seventeenth Century Dutch Genre Paintings* and in his work on Pieter de Hooch. These art historians tend to believe that many seventeenth-century viewers, well-read and classically educated, found in still-life paintings religious and moral "messages" that might escape their twentieth- and twenty-first-century counterparts.

Others, especially those influenced by Professor Svetlana Alpers of the University of California at Berkeley and her book, *The Art of Describing*, are inclined to define Dutch paintings as painterly *tours-de-force*, in which attention to technique and formal elements are more important than the search for "hidden" meanings. They see cleverly composed Dutch pictures as visual descriptions of carefully observed phenomena or a fulfillment of the human desire to imitate nature.

Some viewers, including specialized scholars, categorize these paintings as "visual documents"—evidence of aspects of Dutch cultural life. Still others are intrigued with the notion of art serving to entertain and bring visual pleasure and delight rather than to instruct.

Controversy abounds about the interpretation of Dutch and Flemish works. Oscar Mandel (1996) sharply criticizes those who spend too much time looking for veiled or hidden moralistic, didactic, salacious, or erotic meanings embedded in Dutch imagery. British art historian Christopher Brown generally seems to agree. "Genre paintings are not sermons, religious tracts, or moral emblems," he observes. "Rather they are precisely what they seem to be, carefully chosen and constructed accounts of everyday life, which were valued by contemporaries for the familiarity of their subject-matter and the skill of their makers" (1999).

In this volume, a number of interpretations are suggested, often by posing a question, but the viewer is left with a choice of plausible meanings for the depictions. Invariably, whether we speak of seventeenth-century viewers or today's modern viewers, meaning is made by the perceiver. Artists had, and still have, little control over what personalized sense viewers make of imagery.

Meaning, like beauty, is in the eye of the beholder, so feast your eyes, savor these images either as foods for thought or seductive sensory appeals to your appetites and tastes, but most especially, enjoy this delicious assortment.

Donna R. Barnes, Ed.D.
Professor, Hofstra University

DUTCH FOODWAYS:
AN AMERICAN CONNECTION

Matters of Taste provides a framework for seventeenth-century Dutch foodways by discussing contemporary food preparation, the way food was served and enjoyed, and the important part food played in holidays and other festive occasions. Food and drink, kitchen implements, and cooks are all depicted in the still-life pictures and genre scenes produced by the Dutch Masters during the Netherlands' Golden Age. These portrayals illustrate the diet and food customs of a vibrant culture and document the food connections between the Netherlands and its North American colony, New Netherland. The paintings also reveal a great deal about Dutch agriculture, horticulture, and husbandry while showing their relevance to the American kitchen today.

Although the lowland countries of Belgium and the Netherlands have been linked throughout history by geography, the Dutch culture, and a common language, it is important to note that the Belgian and Dutch cuisines now differ. Belgium's kitchen, akin to that of France, is known for its exuberant bistro-style foods, presently in vogue in America. Dutch cuisine is more staid, but the fine foods grown and produced in the Netherlands, especially its vegetables and cheeses, are sought after all over the world.

OVERVIEW OF DUTCH CULINARY HISTORY FROM
THE MIDDLE AGES UNTIL THE SEVENTEENTH CENTURY

The earliest printed cookbook in the Dutch language, *Een Notabel Boecxken van Cokeryen* (A notable little book of cookery), was published circa 1514. The presumed author and publisher, Thomas van der Noot, belonged to a prominent Brussels' family. Van der Noot's book was meant for the nobility, high-placed clergy, and wealthy bourgeoisie, for only these classes could afford the expensive foodstuffs it called for. As was common practice then, many of the 170 or so recipes were copied from other sources, especially from the famous French cookbook of the period, *Le Viandier*. *Een Notabel Boecxken van Cokeryen* includes recipes for sauces, fish dishes, meats, poultry, game, and eggs, as well as for raised pies, tarts, and sweets. The recipes are clearly divided into dishes for everyday consumption and those to be eaten on the church-ordained days of fasting and abstinence, when meat, dairy products, and eggs were forbidden. This prohibition applied about 150 days a year, when only fish, vegetables, herbs, fruits (including dried fruits and nuts), legumes, oils, salt, spices, sugar, honey, beer, wine, grain products, and bread were permitted. These rules were far more stringent than the ones American Roman Catholics practiced until the mid-1960s.

Eggs, said to be the poor man's supper, were particularly popular in the Netherlands. They were often barely cooked and then slurped from the shell.

During the Middle Ages, milk was not drunk as it is today, in part because it spoiled quickly and was thought to be unhealthy, so much so that after drinking it one was advised to rinse one's mouth with honey! Instead it was cooked in porridges, or custards, some of which had a pastry base.

Milk was also preserved as butter and as the less perishable cheese. In both of the Low Countries, unlike other parts of Europe, butter rather than oil was used. Several varieties of cheese, made from both cows' and sheep's milk, were being manufactured as early as the fourteenth and fifteenth centuries. Cheese was usually named for the place where it originated; the Netherlands is still known for its Gouda and Edam cheeses. Gouda cheese is made from milk with cream and Edam-style cheese is made from skimmed milk. Early on, sheep cheeses were also popular. Often colored green with sheep's feces, these cheeses primarily came from the northern island of Texel or the town of 's Gravenzande. As breeding methods improved and milk production increased, more recipes appeared for milk products, including home made ricotta-like cheeses.

Pork was the favorite meat of all classes. Pigs were everywhere and generally roamed free. In the fall, pigs were slaughtered, and families who could afford it would purchase a cow for slaughter as well. Both were salted and smoked for winter consumption (see cat. 34). By the end of the sixteenth century, cattle, particularly oxen, were imported from Denmark and Schleswig-Holstein in northern Germany, to be fattened for slaughter in the grassy meadows of the northern Netherlands. Chickens, ducks, and geese were the common poultry, although songbirds were eaten as well (see cat. 48).

The nobility had the privilege of hunting both large and small game animals, including deer, wild boar, rabbits, pheasants, partridge, bittern, cranes, swans, heron, and ducks. Falcons and sparrow hawks were trained to retrieve partridge, geese, ducks, kites, and doves, or any other fowl. By the fifteenth century, game was usually reserved for feasts rather than the daily table of the noblemen.

It is often implied that medieval people strongly seasoned their foods because meat was generally spoiled, an unlikely premise since many government regulations concerned the sale of meat and people knew about preservation methods like drying, smoking, and salting. Seasoning was, as it is now, more a matter of taste. Spices from the Orient, such as pepper, nutmeg, cloves and cinnamon, were introduced by way of Venice and became status symbols for the well-to-do. These spices were mixed with sour verjuice (juice from unripe grapes or apples) and locally grown herbs such as parsley, sage, or savory. They gave the dishes a sharply spiced and sour taste, which was much appreciated.

Little is known about the sustenance of the masses in the Middle Ages, since the body of knowledge about food of the period comes from records of the elaborate banquets held by the nobility for weddings, victories, or coronations. These extravagant medieval feasts consisted of several courses, each containing ten or more dishes, and were also known for their between-course events. At one of Philip of Burgundy's banquets, an entire orchestra stepped out of a raised pie and started to play!

Fishing was as important to the food supply as it was to the economy. In the fifteenth century, when large schools of herring moved closer to the Netherlands, the Dutch herring fishery boomed. The invention of *haring kaken* (the cleaning and salting of herring on board ship) made the fish less perishable and therefore available as a major trade good. Salt, also used to preserve meat, was imported from France and Portugal. Herring and dried cod were the chief fish eaten by all Dutch classes and were especially important on days of fasting and abstinence. Eel were abundant in the rivers, as were carp, pike, and bream. These freshwater fish were preferred by the more affluent, while the poor and working class ate dried plaice, flounder, or whiting.

Castles and cloisters were the centers of horticulture at the beginning of the Middle Ages, and their gardens provided vegetables, herbs, fruits, and nuts. Gradually, however, the increased mercantile influence of the large towns (such as Antwerp and Amsterdam) and their expanding markets allowed horticulture to begin to flourish beyond the estates of the nobility and clergy. By the sixteenth century, the Netherlands was known throughout Europe for its vegetables (see cat. 18). To extend the growing season, seeds were cultivated under glass in cold frames. In 1556, Gheeraert Vorselman's *Een Nyeuwen Coock Boeck* (A new cookbook) was the first to publish salad and vegetable recipes.

In the Middle Ages wheat, rye, barley, oats, peas, and beans were grown. However, the Netherlands did not grow enough grain to supply its inhabitants, so large quantities of grain were imported, mostly from eastern Prussia and Poland. The grain trade developed early, and by the fifteenth century it was concentrated in Amsterdam. Bread was one of the mainstays of the diet. The more expensive wheat bread (called white bread) was eaten by the affluent. Rye bread (called black bread) was the usual food of the poor.

Beer was the common drink, although wine was favored by the well-to-do and buttermilk was popular on the farms. Beer was brewed at home, but as early as the fourteenth century, the cities of Haarlem and Amersfoort had famous breweries. Cloisters, too, were known for their brews and some of the famous present-day Belgian beers date back to that tradition.

Abundant feasts at times of plenty contrasted with the famines of the Middle Ages, which wiped out large parts of the population. The Dutch were true trenchermen, who would eat and drink immoderately at parties and banquets for guild celebrations, weddings, or births (where they would "drown the child" in frequent toasts), or at funerals (called in jest "grave weddings"). Paintings by Breughel and other artists of the period depict such events.

However, the regular meal pattern consisted, at most, of two meals a day with two dishes for the main meal served around eleven in the morning and one dish for the evening meal, served just before going to bed. Bread, cheese, root vegetables, garlic, onions, peas, beans, fruit in season, porridge, eggs, and a little meat or fish, when available, were the main foodstuffs. Toward the end of the Middle Ages, mealtimes shifted and, increasingly, breakfast was added as the third meal of the day.

Before all meals hands were washed, for which a water pitcher, bowl, and towel or napkin were provided. Plates were first dried slices of bread, replaced by wooden trenchers and eventually tin dishes. The table was covered with a cloth with bread and salt placed upon it. Fingers, spoons, or knives were used for eating. Forks were not used until the end of the seventeenth century.

A major change in eating habits occurred in the middle of the sixteenth century, after the Protestant Reformation, when the northern provinces of the Netherlands largely embraced the Protestant faith, as preached by John Calvin, and the southern provinces remained Roman

Catholic. It may be assumed that the Protestants abandoned the days of abstinence immediately, although they continued to eat fish on Friday. The Catholic obligation to fast was difficult and expensive, causing some medievalists to believe this could be one of the reasons for the success of the Reformation. It is worth noting that most olive oil-producing countries remained Catholic and most butter-producing countries became Protestant.

FOOD AND DRINK IN THE NETHERLANDS DURING THE SEVENTEENTH CENTURY

Daily meals and customary beverages

The seventeenth century brought the great prosperity, known as the "Golden Age." Both the East and West India Companies were founded in its first quarter, allowing Dutch ships to bring spices from the Dutch East Indies (now Indonesia) and sugar from first Brazil and then plantations in the West Indies. Exotic plants, such as the pineapple, were brought from every port where Dutch ships docked. With more food available, consumption increased and the common eating pattern grew to four meals a day. Breakfast consisted of bread with butter or cheese; the noon meal, of a stew of meat and vegetables, or of fish, with fruit, cooked vegetables, honey cake, or raised pie. The afternoon meal of bread with butter or cheese was eaten a few hours later. Just before bedtime, leftovers from noon, or bread with butter or cheese, or porridge were served.

The Dutch were known for their love of sweets, sweet breads like honey cake or ginger bread, and confections like marzipan, candied almonds, or cinnamon bark, which were consumed in addition to the daily fare. Like their cheeses, the Dutch *koek* (honey cake), akin to ginger bread, was named for its city of origin. By the fifteenth century, *Deventer koek* from the town of Deventer in the eastern Netherlands was already famous throughout the land. Waffles, wafers, *olie-koecken* (deep-fried balls of dough with raisins, apples, and almonds that became a forerunner of the donut), and pancakes were some of the celebratory foods both prepared at home and sold on the streets, as contemporary artists portray (see cats. 41 and 50).

Beer continued to be the common drink. Because water was boiled in its preparation, beer was a safer drink than plain water, which was often polluted. Buttermilk was often drunk on the farm. The sweeter and less perishable wines from the Mediterranean countries were popular with the upper classes. Young white wines, imported from France and Germany, were at that time very sour, so they were mixed with honey and spices such as cloves, coriander, cinnamon, and ginger to make a sweet drink like hippocras, which was enjoyed by the upper classes at the end of a large meal.

In the latter half of the seventeenth century tea and coffee made a significant impact on meal patterns and social customs. An early tea cargo in 1610 was considered a curiosity, but shipments gradually increased and domestic markets developed. Tea preparation required its own paraphernalia like small porcelain tea bowls and teapots, also imported from the Orient. Many humorous tales exist about the quantity consumed at popular late-seventeenth-century tea parties, where purportedly, between twenty and one hundred small cupfuls per person were drunk. Tea was served with sweets such as hard candies, marzipan, and cookies, particularly a Utrecht specialty called *theerandjes* (literally, "tea edges," or strips), made from a clove-flavored dough topped with candied orange peel and citron (see cookbook). The third meal of the day, which earlier in the century had consisted of bread and butter, was incorporated into the tea ritual and moved to the late afternoon.

During teatime, women would gather in small groups, which had a certain cachet. Coffee, however, was a more public drink. It was enjoyed in coffeehouses, where men would stop in to have a cup, smoke a pipe, and read the paper. Stephanus Blankaart, an Amsterdam physician and author of a 1633 book on diet, comments on the large crowds visiting the coffeehouses in his city.

Diet of the poor and working class

The poor had a much more limited diet. In some parts of the country daily meals consisted of not much more than whole kernel rye (black) bread, amounting to some five pounds a day for a family of four. The remarkably complete account books of the Amsterdam Municipal Orphanage provide more insight into the diet of the poor (the orphans), and the working or lower middle class (the staff). Milk, fish, rice, groats (hulled grain of barley, oats, or buckwheat), peas, beans, rye, wheat, pork, butter, cheese, beer, and miscellaneous items such as treacle, salt, dried fruits, and spices were purchased for their daily meals. As noted in the menu for the year 1640, the orphans were fed two meals a day. The noon meal consisted of different varieties of beans and peas and a second dish of salted or smoked meat, or sausage with groats and raisins, bacon with carrots or cabbage, salt cod, herring, or dried cod. All of the meals were served with bread. The evening repast invariably consisted of a kind of porridge—rice porridge or groats cooked with buttermilk, buttermilk with rye bread, bread and treacle cooked together, buttermilk and wheat bread cooked together, or buttermilk cooked with barley. The main difference between the diets of the orphans and the staff was quantity. The adult staff was given more bread (especially wheat bread) and more meat.

Diet of the wealthy middle and upper classes

With fortunes made in overseas trade, well-to-do families built country houses away from their city dwellings and places of business. The country houses had gardens where fruits and vegetables were grown for home consumption. Plants from far away lands were also cultivated. The paintings in this book provide a startling insight into how many New World foodstuffs and plants had been integrated into the Dutch market and lifestyle by this period (see cats. 13 and 44).

The definitive Dutch cookbook of the seventeenth century was the anonymously written *De Verstandige Kock* (The sensible cook). The author of this essay included a translation of *De Verstandige Kock* in her book *The Sensible Cook: Dutch Foodways in the Old and the New World*, Syracuse University Press, 1989 and 1998. Originally incorporated into a book on gardening by Pieter van Aengelen and published by Marcus Doornick in 1667, it later formed part of a larger collective book, *Het Vermakelijck Landtleven* (The pleasurable country life). Unless otherwise attributed, all quotations in this book are taken from the 1683 edition of this work, also published by Marcus Doornick.

De Verstandige Kock gives recipes for the homegrown bounty of the rising middle and upper classes. Like the cookbooks of previous centuries, it was written for the rapidly expanding wealthy upper class, which had become the leading segment of Dutch society as the power of the nobility waned. *De Verstandige Kock* begins with salads and continues with recipes for vegetables, meat, game, and poultry, salted, smoked, and dried fish, saltwater and freshwater fish, and baked goods such as raised pies and tarts. Separate chapters on preserving meats and fruits end the volume. The book gives the impression that the daily fare of the wealthy was plentiful and varied.

Bread as the mainstay of the diet

Bread was consumed with butter or cheese for breakfast, paired with meat or *hutspot* (a one-pot dish of meats and vegetables) for the midday main meal, and served with, or as a part of, the porridge at night. Special baked goods followed the human life cycle, from *zottinnekoecken* (pastries akin to rusks; literally, "crazy woman's cakes" or "airhead" cakes for their light texture), which were served filled with sugared comfits for celebrations of births (see cat. 33), to *doot coeckjes*, or funeral cookies, the recipe for which appears in the handwritten cookbook of Maria Sanders van Rensselaer (1749–1830), wife of Philip van Rensselaer of Cherry Hill, Albany. In the seventeenth century the poor and working class continued to eat rye or coarse wheat bread; daily consumption of white bread was a symbol of affluence, as the paintings often testify (see cat. 5).

Rye and wheat were the main grain ingredients for bread baking. Rye, grown in the drier eastern and southern provinces, produced a dark (black) bread (see cat. 47). Wheat, mostly imported, produced a lighter bread with softer crumb, or, when finely sifted, a finely textured white bread (see cat. 5). In the workroom, often behind his shop, the baker mixed the flour, salt, yeast, and water into dough, which was then kneaded to the right consistency. Wheat dough was kneaded by hand; the heavier rye dough was kneaded in a trough with the feet. By government regulation, hands or feet were not to be washed with soap, but with hot water, then rubbed with flour.

Bread dough was shaped in various ways (see cats. 3 and 4) and sometimes flavored with nutmeg, cloves, and especially cinnamon, or filled with dried fruits and decorated with sugar, or even gold leaf. Each baker also placed his own identification mark on his products. It was not the bakers who set the price for their bread, but the local government. Part of a government's task was to ensure sufficient food to protect the population from famine. Seventeenth-century municipal governments regulated the size, weight, and price of bread by appointing inspectors to oversee its production. Bread prices were established in relation to grain prices. Rye bread had stable weights of six and twelve pounds, but its price would vary (*zetting*). For white bread, the price would be stable, but the weight would vary (*rijding*). Prices and weights were announced in bulletins affixed to prominent structures in town.

Bakers were organized into guilds, which petitioned the government on behalf of their membership and regulated and curtailed the bakers' trade. These necessary restrictions ensured an adequate market share for each bakery. To be a full member of the baker's guild, one had to be a citizen of the town, complete an apprenticeship, and pass the baker's exam.

FOOD AND DRINK IN NEW NETHERLAND

Every day Americans eat dishes that can be traced back to the foodways brought to New Netherland by the early Dutch settlers, who planted fruit trees (among them apples, pears and peaches), vegetables such as lettuces, cabbages, parsnips, carrots, and beets, and herbs such as parsley, rosemary, chives, and tarragon. Farm animals, particularly horses, pigs, and cows, were among the most valuable imported commodities.

Adriaen van der Donck, a graduate of the University of Leiden with a doctorate in civil and canon law, came to New Netherland in 1641 to become *schout* (sheriff) for Patroon Kiliaen van Rensselaer (c. 1585–1643) in Rensselaerswijck (now Albany and Rensselaer Counties). He wrote A *Description of the New Netherlands* (first published in 1655) to entice his fellow countrymen to settle in the new colony. Van der Donck reported that all sorts of European fruits and vegetables "thrive well," and marveled at the abundance of native fish, fowl, and other wild life (1968).

Trade with the Indians was an important aspect of life in New Netherland. The Dutch traded cloth, beads, and ironware such as axes and cooking kettles for beaver skins and also used their baking skills to produce breads, sweet breads, and cookies as commodities. The Indians valued Dutch wheat bread, which had been previously unknown to them. Whereas in the Netherlands most of the wheat was imported, in the Rensselaerswijck patroonship, wheat became the most important cash crop. Evidently bakers were using so much flour for the lucrative Indian trade that not enough was left to bake bread for the Dutch community. A 1649 ordinance for Fort Orange and the village of Beverwijck (now Albany) forbade further baking of bread and cookies for Native Americans. There was even a record of a court case in which a baker was fined because "a certain savage" was seen coming out of his house "carrying an oblong sugar bun." At mid-century, the bakers signed a petition to organize a guild, but they were denied, and no guilds were ever established in New Netherland.

In their new colony, the settlers continued to prepare familiar foods. From ship records we know that West India Company ships supplied them with kitchen tools, such as frying pans to fry their favorite pancakes, (see cat. 57) or the irons to make their waffles and wafers (see cookbook). As diaries and inventories note, the settlers themselves brought the implements used for cooking these familiar foods, duplicating life in the Netherlands as best as they could. Cookbooks of their descendants show that they continued their own foodways but also incorporated native foods into their daily diet, albeit in ways that were familiar to them. For instance, they made pumpkin cornmeal pancakes, pumpkin sweetmeat, or added cranberries instead of the usual raisins and apples to their favorite *olie-koecken*. Lovers of porridge found it easy to get used to *sapaen* (Indian cornmeal mush), but they added milk to it. This dish became such an integral part of the Dutch American diet that it is mentioned under the heading of National Dishes on an 1830 menu for the Saint Nicholas' Day Dinner held at the American Hotel in Albany. Cookies, pancakes, waffles, wafers, *olie-koecken*, pretzels, and coleslaw are some of the dishes that were brought to America by the Dutch colonists. While the Dutch period of New Netherland only lasted officially from 1609 to 1664, the Dutch influence, particularly the culinary influence, persists to this day.

FOODS FOR SPECIAL OCCASIONS IN THE NETHERLANDS AND NEW NETHERLAND

The seventeenth-century Dutch celebrated four winter holidays: Saint Nicholas' Day on December sixth, Christmas, New Year's, and Epiphany (Twelfth Night, or the Feast of the Three Kings) on January sixth. For children, Saint Nicholas' Day was the most important, and the traditions from this celebration have been absorbed into our American Christmas festivities. Virtually nothing is certain about the real Saint Nicholas. His legend may have grown out of life stories of several bishops by that name. According to tradition, he was a fourth-century bishop of Myra, in Asia Minor, who became associated with anonymous gift-giving. Saint Nicholas was also the patron saint of sailors, who brought his cult via the sea routes from Eastern to Western Europe. In the Low Countries, he was often the main character in the miracle plays performed in town squares. This made him less a venerated saint and more of a popular figure. He became the *kindervriend*, or children's friend, who brought presents and sweet treats to the small folk. The latter included *duivekaters* (holiday bread; see cat. 4), candied cinnamon bark, or flat, chewy honey cake formed in a wooden mold. He was so much a part of yearly family celebrations that even during the Reformation the *Kinderfeest* (children's feast), could not be eradicated by government and Protestant church officials.

In the beginning of the nineteenth century, the American novelist Washington Irving (1783–1859), observing the Saint Nicholas' Day celebrations by his Dutch American neighbors, borrowed its central figure and made him part of the American Christmas festivities. He changed the tall, thin, stern-but-just bishop into our short, rotund, and jolly Santa Claus. Nineteenth-century illustrators created further embellishments to his appearance, while different ethnic groups added their traditions, and the result was the secular component of the American Christmas celebration.

In the Netherlands, the religious holidays such as Christmas, Easter, and Pentecost were (and still are) celebrated for two days. Deacons' records of the Dutch Reformed Church show they were celebrated this way in New Netherland as well.

New Year's Eve was especially noisy, with the firing of guns to bring in the New Year. Ordinances in both the Netherlands and New Netherland eventually prohibited such behavior. The special treat for New Year's Day in the Netherlands was *nieuwjaarskoeken* (thin, crisp wafers), which originated in the eastern part of the country and adjoining parts of Germany. These wafers were made in a special wafer iron. The oblong or round long-handled irons, made by blacksmiths, created imprints of a religious or secular nature on the wafers. Wafer irons were often given as a wedding gift, even in this country. Enormous quantities of wafers were prepared on New Year's Day. They were consumed by family, servants, and guests and distributed to children, who went from house to house singing New Year's songs, while collecting their share of treats along the way. There is ample evidence in diaries and letters that Dutch Americans continued the custom of visiting each other on New Year's Day. In New Netherland, however, the *nieuwjaarskoeken* were molded in wooden cake-boards, instead of wafer irons (see recipes in the handwritten cookbooks of Elizabeth Ann Breese Morse [d. 1828] and Maria Lott Lefferts [1786–1865] of Brooklyn). The American New Year's cake is a combination of two Dutch pastries brought here by the early settlers, the *nieuwjaarskoeken* described above and spiced, chewy, honey cakes formed in a wooden mold or cake-board. It was in the late eighteenth century that this homemade pastry prepared in heirloom wafer irons by the Dutch, changed to a mostly store-bought product purchased by the population at large. Bakers found it much more expedient to roll out the dough, imprint it with a cake-board, cut it out, and bake it. Because the pastry was not connected with a religious celebration, most groups easily adopted it.

Food historian Stephen Schmidt holds that Americans became acquainted with Dutch cookies through *nieuwjaarskoeken*, bringing the word *cookie* into American English (see cat. 41). Recipes for cookies appeared for the first time in the earliest published American cookbook, compiled by Amelia Simmons in 1796. Cake-boards developed into a unique kind of folk art, similar to their counterparts in the Netherlands, recording important events of the time, political figures, or the American eagle.

The last Dutch winter holiday, Epiphany, did not leave a lasting mark on American life. In the Netherlands it was a rather rowdy occasion, celebrated within the family circle with waffles and pancakes served as the standard fare (see cat. 51).

The spring religious feast of Easter was celebrated in some parts of the Netherlands with large bonfires and most everywhere with the consumption of Easter eggs. No specific mention of Easter (other than the collection of offerings by the deacons of the Dutch Reformed Church) has been found in New Netherland.

Pinkster, Pentecost, or Whitsuntide, the third most important holiday in the Christian calendar which occurs fifty days after Easter, was celebrated in the Netherlands as well as in New Netherland. In the Old World, the secular festivities associated with Pinksteren, as it is now called, were a kind of combined May Day and fertility celebration. To foster a good harvest, a young girl was chosen as the *Pinksterblom* (Pinkster flower) and was carried around bedecked with flowers by the children of the town, who collected coins to buy treats. New Netherland diaries relate how the Dutch settlers gave their slaves the day off and everyone frolicked and ate large quantities of eggs. After the Revolution and in the beginning of the nineteenth century, the holiday tended to be a celebration for African Americans. New York City, where freed slaves had arrived in large numbers, was especially known for its lavish Pinkster festivals, and in Albany Pinkster is said to have lasted a whole week.

In both the Netherlands and New Netherland, there were many additional events associated with special foods. These include yearly fairs, where waffles, wafers, and *olie-koecken* were sold; the birth of a child, with its special drink of *kandeel* (wine with eggs and spices); and weddings, where guests feasted on the best the household had to offer. That even funerals were part of the well-defined culinary customs of the colony may be gleaned from the recipes for *doot coeckjes* (funeral cookies) and spiced wine of Maria Sanders van Rensselaer (1749–1830). At all festivities the Dutch proved to be truly hearty eaters. For example, a typical three-course feast to mark the accession to office of two Groningen professors featured turkey, hare, haunch of mutton, ham, veal, and half a lamb, all served with bread, butter, cheese, mustard, anchovies, lemons, and wine. It is telling, therefore, that Adriaen van der Donck, who served as sheriff in Rensselaerswijck, specifically noted that Native Americans "have no excessive eaters or gluttons among them" (1968).

IMPLEMENTS AND HOUSEHOLD OBJECTS

The paintings in this volume show many of the common implements of a seventeenth-century kitchen. Kettles, in various sizes and usually made from brass, were hung over the fire and used for boiling water, or for cooking food in liquid (see cat. 45). Cooking pots—tall, earthenware vessels with narrow necks—were also used for cooking with liquids and so were their bronze or brass successors with typical triangular handles (see cat. 60). Braising or stewing pans were covered with a lid to trap the steam for cooking with a limited amount of liquid (see cats. 27 and 36). Frying pans were used for cooking over high heat with a small amount of fat (see cats. 36 and 50). A spit with dripping pan was used for roasting. A *taert-panne* (Dutch oven) served as a small portable oven for baking the sweet and savory raised pies. Its lipped lid allowed coals to be heaped on top so that the pie would be heated from above and below (see cat. 54). A gridiron, which was placed over hot coals to roast flat pieces of meat or fish or to toast bread to be grated and used to thicken sauces, is not shown, but its use is implied in some of the recipes (see cookbook). The waffles in several paintings represent the use of a waffle iron. A rasp, sieve, colander, mortar and pestle, and skimmer are portrayed, as well as knives and spoons. Plates, platters, cups, glasses, bowls, pots, bottles, basins for storage, and a *vleeschkuyp* (a wooden tub for pickling meat; see cat. 45) round out the implement list for a well-equipped seventeenth-century kitchen. At the end of the century the very wealthy began to furnish their guests with eating implements, including a knife and spoon and the newer fork. However, several decades elapsed before the fork was generally accepted; many people claimed it was unnecessary because, in the common phrase, "God has given us fingers."

COOKBOOKS

The cookbooks handed down in Dutch American families prove that the colonists maintained their familiar foodways for generations. Their recipes are found in handwritten cookbooks spanning three centuries. More than thirty such cookbooks, belonging to descendants of the Dutch settlers of New Netherland, who retained their culinary ethnicity by handing down their special recipes, have been identified.

From some of the families only a single book remains, such as the undated "Mrs. Lefferts' Book," handwritten by Maria Lott Lefferts of Brooklyn, or that of Elizabeth Ann Breese Morse [d. 1828], entitled "Mrs. E. A. Morse, Her Book, April 10, 1805." Not surprisingly, the wealthiest families—the Van Cortlandts of the lower Hudson Valley, the Van Rensselaers of Albany, and the Dutch families in the New Paltz area—have left the richest assortment.

There are five Van Cortlandt manuscripts; the two most important belonged to Anna de Peyster (1701–1774) and to Anne Stevenson van Cortlandt (1774–1821) and her mother, Magdalena Douw (1750–1817). The Van Rensselaer family was amazingly prolific in its record-keeping. Its members produced at least twelve handwritten books over five generations, spanning almost two hundred years. That of Maria Sanders van Rensselaer (1749–1830) is the earliest, followed by those of her daughter Arriet (1775–1840) and her granddaughter Elizabeth (1799–1835).

Manuscripts of lesser-known families have also survived. A manuscript by Anna Maria Elting of New Paltz is dated May 18th, 1819. "Hylah Hasbrouck's Receipts," also from New Paltz and dated 1840, includes a recipe for *condale*, or *kandeel*, the customary drink celebrating the birth of a child. The same recipe appears in an unidentified book dated July 5th, 1849. Hybertie Pruyn (1873–1964) of Albany and even Washington Irving had several recipes among their papers.

In this span of three hundred and fifty years, recipes changed, partially because the fine details of the methods were forgotten, but also because modern equipment replaced old utensils, or new ingredients such as baking powder were invented. Not only did the recipes evolve, but also their names became more and more Anglicized. *Krullen* (curls), a curl-shaped deep-fried pastry, became *crulla*, *crullar*, and ended up as today's *cruller*, or donut. In the handwritten cookbooks, waffles are frequently spelled phonetically in Dutch as *wafuls*. Another good example is coleslaw. The origin of this cabbage salad is, apparently, completely forgotten, yet the name comes simply from the Dutch *kool* for cabbage, and *sla* for slaw or salad. The widest variety of spellings found was for the seventeenth century *olie-koecken*, a word that has changed even in the Netherlands, where the pastry is now called *oliebollen* (oil-balls). The Dutch American spelling ranges from *oelykoeks* or *ollykoeks*, through *ole cook* to *oly cook* (see cookbook for two versions).

CONCLUSION

To answer questions on how seventeenth-century foods actually tasted, a separate cookbook has been included. This practical component contains the modern versions of all the Dutch and Dutch colonial recipes noted in the main volume of *Matters of Taste*. A few extra recipes have been added to complete the story of Dutch foodways. The cookbook provides recipes that today's cook can use to serve up intriguing and enticing tastes of the past.

Peter G. Rose
Food Historian

CATALOG

I   Circle of Pieter Aertsen

Market Scene

Dutch, early seventeenth century

oil on canvas; 41¾ x 54½ inches

Collection of Hofstra Museum, Hofstra University, Hempstead, New York

THIS MARKET SCENE features men and women engaged in the daily shopping ritual. The women's pleated millstone collars suggest the painting probably dates to the early seventeenth century.

Among the items for sale is a live piglet held by the old woman. She also clutches a brace of birds, suspended by their beaks. Another person is carrying a live rooster. The market woman, wearing a red jacket, holds a goose. The affluent-looking couple at center is inspecting a dead hare. Behind them, a young woman in white cradles a live chicken. She looks out toward the viewer, inviting appreciation of this market's plentitude . . . and possibly her available beauty? The man with the tall crowned hat supports a live turkey. The people holding livestock are either sellers or consumers.

Atop the sales table are dead birds, ducks, pigs' feet, eggs, and asparagus. A carp lies in a shallow wooden bowl, next to white onions, leaf lettuces, and artichokes.

The cityscape background, featuring clock- and step-gabled buildings, suggests a Dutch or Flemish locale. A shop window is open to reveal rounds of cheese. Nearby, a market woman sits with her basket and a snoozing dog.

Market scenes were prized by both Dutch and Flemish art buyers, who savored the talents of the painters as much as the abundant foods available to discerning and affluent households. The identity of the painter remains a puzzle. Although Pieter Aertsen (c. 1507–1575) and Joachim Beuckelaer (c. 1533–c. 1575) are jointly credited with having initiated market and kitchen scenes, as important genre themes for the still-life display of vegetables, fruits, fish, meat, and game, their "characters" are typically more animated. Likewise, their styles and compositions differ; none of the religious or erotic elements found in many of their market scenes are present here.

This picture, nonetheless, points to Aertsen's influence, anticipating later seventeenth-century developments in Dutch and Flemish specialized market scenes (see cats. 8, 11, 18, 44, and 59) where fish stalls, poultry markets, game sellers, and fruit and vegetable vendors are depicted as separate entities.   DRB

HIDDEN AMONG the abundance of the market stall's foodstuffs is a bunch of green asparagus, an unusual sight in a painting from this period. Although *Asparagus Officinalis* has many varieties, among them white, green, and purple types, deep-planted white asparagus were far more frequently shown in Dutch paintings. This white variety, with its almost meaty flavor and steak-like price, is a *primeur*, a seasonal vegetable in the Netherlands in early spring, and is now primarily grown in the southern provinces of Brabant and especially Limburg. In the New World, Adriaen van der Donck, in his *Description of the New Netherlands* of 1655, lists asparagus in the herb garden (1968). A graduate of the University of Leiden with a doctorate in civil and canon law, Van der Donck came to New Netherland in 1641 to become *schout* for Patroon Kiliaen van Rensselaer (c. 1585–1643) in Rensselaerswijck (presently Albany and Rensselaer Counties). Seeds for all sorts of plants were brought by the first Dutch settlers and also shipped back and forth between the colony and the homeland.

The author of *De Verstandige Kock*, the definitive Dutch cookbook of the seventeenth century, was well aware that asparagus should not be overcooked. The recipe reads: "Asparagus are just boiled, not too well done, and then eaten with oil and vinegar, and pepper, or otherwise with melted butter and grated nutmeg." Another popular way of serving asparagus can be found in the cookbook.   PGR

2 Osias Beert, the Elder (c. 1580–1623)
Fruits, Nuts, Wine, and Sweets on a Ledge

Flemish, c. 1610
oil on panel; 32¾ x 25⅛ inches
Teresa Heinz and the late Senator John Heinz

THIS INVITING ARRAY of desserts is arranged on a wooden table. A pewter plate is brimming with walnuts and hazelnuts. A Wan-li porcelain bowl contains apples, peaches, and apricots. Flies have been attracted to the fruit and a butterfly hovers nearby. A *façon de Venise* (in the style of Venice) goblet holds red wine. A matching pewter dish of shelled almonds, raisins, and dried figs is seen through the ornate *glasbokaal* (covered wine decanter) containing white wine. Ripe figs, a splint box of quince paste, baked pastry confections, and sugared comfits are near a knife, its porcelain hoof-shaped handle projecting over the table's edge.

Beert's harmoniously restrained use of browns, yellows, and reds, set against a black background with black and white accents on the butterfly and knife handle gives this *pronk* still life considerable grace.

Can this picture be classified as a *vanitas*, a reminder of fleeting earthly pleasures and sensory delights? Sugared candies have been associated with rich men's meals from the early 1600s. Flies are attracted to foods that rot. Everything here is perishable, like mankind. Is the viewer being admonished to live moderately as "*Alte veel is ongesont*" (too much is unhealthy)? Perhaps the artist deliberately chose elements that resonated with Christian significance, including walnuts, whose meats alluded to Christ? The butterfly might have symbolized Christ's Resurrection, since the insect emerges anew from its tomb-like chrysalis. Fruit could be interpreted as a symbol of the Tree of Knowledge in the Garden of Eden. Does the hoofed knife handle suggest a knight, choosing between spiritual and mundane concerns? Or is this simply a feast for the eyes that invites the viewer to revel in the artist's mastery of painterly techniques? Perhaps the carefully delineated fly is meant to call attention to the artist's ability to create objects from differing visual perspectives. The viewer, like the fly, is invited to come closer and examine each succulent sweet.   DRB

NUTS, FRESH AND DRIED FRUIT, candied quince, candied (Jordan) almonds, and cinnamon bark are only some of the sweet seductions offered to lead us astray. The platter of pastries contains a cookie akin to biscotti, hand-shaped tartlets, and pastry dough letters molded before baking.

The intriguing edible alphabet is still an integral part of the Saint Nicholas' Day celebration in the Netherlands. Letters made from puff pastry dough filled with almond paste and chocolate letters representing the initials of the recipient are today's traditional gifts for the December feast. In the painting, the letters and tartlets, made by professional pastry bakers, are both decorated with gold leaf. While there is no direct evidence that such finely decorated wares were baked in New Netherland, a recipe for almond tartlets in the handwritten cookbook of Anna de Peyster (1701–1774), maternal aunt of Pierre van Cortlandt (1721–1814), indicates that hers were shaped in patty pans and decorated with "green citron" (n.d.). *De Verstandige Kock* gives a recipe for the tartlets' crust: "Take a quarter pound fine wheat flour, place it in an earthenware pot, bake it in the oven with the bread, then make a dough with the yolks of 2 or 3 eggs and a pint of cream, mix with an eighth of a pound finely crushed loaf-sugar, and this way you will make a short [crust] dough without butter or fat." The last statement is not true of course; there is plenty of fat from the cream in the dough. However, it makes an excellent crust that is as tasty as its filling. See cookbook for modern recipe.   PGR

3 Job Berckheyde (1630–1693)
The Baker

Dutch, c. 1681

oil on canvas, 25 x 20⅞ inches

signed lower left center: "H Berckheyde" (HB in ligature); and monogrammed on the bowl: "HB"

Worcester Art Museum, Worcester, Massachusetts; gift of Mr. and Mrs. Milton P. Higgins, 1975.105

BERCKHEYDE'S BURLY BAKER raises an ox horn to sound the blast alerting his customers that freshly baked bread-stuffs are hot from the oven, and ready for sale. The man's furrowed brow speaks volumes about how hard he worked to reach this rewarding moment in the day. His sleeves have been rolled up to reveal the strong, muscular forearms that knead and shape bread dough. His white shirt is opened at the neck, an indication of heat from the bakery ovens. A light-colored canvas apron is wrapped around his waist.

Berckheyde has framed his baker in a niche, permitting a partial view into the bakery behind him but dramatically highlighting the profusion of baked items on the counter in front of him. Utensils and breads can be seen in the bakery. A pretzel rack hangs by a string from the inside curve of the niche.

This not quite monochromatic picture celebrates the painter's skill in capturing the shapes and textures of the bread items, wicker basket, and baker's clothing. The cracked crusted breads are almost lifelike. Could it also be Job Berckheyde's subtle reminder to his contemporaries to give thanks for one's daily bread? If the small vine growing along the niche is a grape leaf, it might allude to the bread and wine of the Eucharist. But if it is ivy, the vine might speak of the naturalness of ingredients needed to make bread. Either interpretation might have satisfied Berck-heyde's viewers.

Berckheyde seems to have been fond of this subject (see cat. 4). Bakers displaying their wares, often sounding a horn, are found in at least seven known seventeenth-century Dutch paintings.   DRB

A MULTIPEGGED RACK was the customary place to hang krakelingen (sweet pretzels). Along the ledge at right, schootjes (portioned rolls) are displayed with two breads of different weights and a basket filled with white, whole wheat, and raisin rolls, rusk-like zottinekoecken (see cat. 40), and more pretzels. The bowl next to the baker might contain a sponge (small portion of risen dough) for the next batch. On the top shelf stands a brass milk jug. More breads are stacked on the shelf below, underscoring the wide variety of bread, or "the royal food," as physician Stephanus Blankaart calls it in his Borgerlijke Tafel (Bourgeois table) (1633).

The custom of horn blowing was brought to New Netherland. In a Beverwijck court case, a baker was fined for blowing his horn and selling white bread at a time of grain scarcity. The Dutch also baked sweet pretzels in the colony and traded them with Native Americans.

In the Netherlands, bakers were organized in guilds and their recipes were a trade secret. The first baking recipes were published in 1753 by "B. G." in Volmaakte Onderrichtinge ten Dienste der Koek-Bakkers of hunne Leerlingen (Perfect in-structions to serve the pastry bakers, or their students). Its recipe for sweet pretzels follows. "Take a pound wheat flour, a pound sugar, a lood [14 grams] cinnamon, 4 lood butter and some potash [baking soda]. Combine it together with the eggs to make a dough and then [shape] 8 pretzels of 3 lood each. Bake on a buttered baking sheet." See cookbook for modern recipe.   PGR

4 Job Berckheyde (1630–1693)
Bakery Shop

Dutch, c. 1680

oil on canvas; 18⅞ x 15½ inches

Allen Memorial Art Museum, Oberlin College, Oberlin, Ohio; R. T. Miller, Jr. Fund, 1956.62

THREE CHILDREN are buying small white cookies from a woman in a bakery shop. The little toddler pays no attention to the transaction but is intent on feeding a treat to a black-and-tan dog, whose tail echoes the curly ribbons in both girls' hairstyles.

A round loaf of bread rests on the counter. A huge *duivekater* rests against a display board on the counter. A wooden pretzel holder with two B-shaped pretzels hangs from the rafters. Behind the shop woman are two shelves, the lower one loaded with rounded breads, the upper one with a brass pail, milk jug, and wicker basket (see cat. 3).

The youngsters are more fashionably dressed than the shopkeeper, whose blue apron covers a plain brown skirt and bodice. Her hair is neatly covered with a white scarf. Her reddish hands indicate her labors. The boy sports a white jabot tied at the neck over a long brown coat, with white shirtsleeves visible under the coat. His brown hose and shoes echo the color of his hair, cascading in curls down his neck, partially covered by a dark hat. His older sister wears a dark dress embroidered with reddish figures and bands at the collar and sleeves, under a brown apron, tied with a bow in the back. The toddler wears a brown-toned bodice over a blouse, and a beige-toned skirt covered with a yellow apron and tied behind the waist.

The picture is suffused with a warm glow, the light entering from the windows and open door at the left. The highly restricted palette of golden brown tones conveys a sense of well-being and tranquility. The painting is visually dominated by the *duivekater*. Did Berckheyde's subject evoke thoughts of St. Nicholas' Day, so beloved by children, or might some viewers have been taken with the importance of the daily bread so tastefully presented here?   DRB

THIS INTERIOR of a bakery shop shows off some of the baker's wares. Among them, large breads, pretzels, and small round sugar cookies. The time must be the holiday season running from the Feast of Saint Nicholas (December sixth) through Epiphany (January sixth), when holiday breads like the prominently displayed *duivekater* were baked, particularly in Amsterdam and North Holland. These breads were shaped with three knobs on the top and bottom and decoratively cut with a sharp knife or razor before baking. Said to resemble a shinbone, some say they were a type of early offering to the gods. The name is equally mysterious and might refer to the devil (*duivel*), or a tomcat (*kater*). Although these breads were probably first made from a rye and honey dough, an Amsterdam ordinance of 1699 indicates that by the end of the seventeenth century they were made from "fine white flour" (Kistemaker 1984). The ordinance forbade their production in times of grain scarcity.

The custom of baking *duivekaters* was brought to the New World. Deacons' records of the Brooklyn Reformed Church show that *duivekaters* were dispensed to the poor on New Year's Day, 1664. Bread recipes remained the trade secret of the bakers. A generic whole wheat bread recipe has been added to the cookbook. It was developed over the years in open-hearth cooking classes and can easily be made in a Dutch oven using a home fireplace.   PGR

5 Abraham van Beyeren (c. 1620–1690)
Peaches, Grapes, Raspberries, Melon, and Wine Glasses

Dutch, c. 1655
oil on panel; 37⅜ x 29⅞ inches
signed in monogram upper right: "AVB"
Private collection

ON A LAID TABLE, covered with a dark cloth, are green and black grapes with leaves, a four-pointed roll, and a large chased silver *tazza* (compote) laden with more grapes, peaches, and red raspberries. A silver gadrooned *plooischotel* (lobed bowl or serving platter) provides the setting for a peach, split apart to reveal its red heart. A *roemer* of white wine, reflecting an image of the artist's studio, and a knife with an agate handle, used to slice a crinkly-skinned melon to reveal its golden flesh and juicy seeds, provide the finishing touches. An elegant *façon de Venise glasbokaal* (covered goblet) has a *bokaaldeksel* (domed cover) decorated with a serpentine coil finial and stem; it is filled with red liquid. These glasses, made by an Italian master glassblower, were in great demand by the affluent Dutch in the mid-seventeenth century. The artist capable of capturing the properties of such goblets, often purchased from a glass house located on the Rozengracht in Amsterdam, was also held in high esteem.

The delicious fruits might have conjured up thoughts of heavenly paradise. The melon was known as a symbol of the need for moderation, but the *tazza* of fruit might have reminded viewers of Roemer Visscher's 1614 emblem of a fruit bowl bearing the moralistic legend "*Vroeg rijp, vroeg rot*" (Early ripe, early rot) as a warning to parents who encouraged precocity in their children. While the riches displayed here might serve as reminders of the fleeting nature of life's pleasures, it is conceivable that viewers were simply taken with the painter's skills. Abraham van Beyeren, who had financial problems, was, perhaps, never able to live amidst these rich man's items. Instead, he might have used them paradoxically in this painting, as a warning against excess and ostentation.   DRB

BEAUTIFUL, RIPE FRUITS are shown off on a silver platter. The raspberries next to the goblet might hint that it contains raspberry liqueur (see cookbook) rather than wine. Liqueurs were consumed at home and sent to New Netherland as trade goods. In 1657, as noted in his correspondence, Jeremias van Rensselaer (1632–1674), the third patroon of Rensselaerswijck, received a "cellar with distilled liquors"—a case with fifteen bottles of cordials (1932). A later shipment contained "anisewater," to be traded for tobacco in New Amsterdam.

It is not surprising to find a crown-shaped white bread roll in the painting's opulent display of expensive objects and foods. White bread was referred to as *herenbrood* (gentlemen's bread). In the Netherlands a spoiled child is called a "white bread child," and the first weeks of marriage, or honeymoon period, are called "the white-bread weeks." Bread, both white and dark, had such an important place in the diet and every day life that it is featured in other expressions as well: when times are hard, "you hang the bread basket high," and when they improve, "there is bread on the [cutting] board."

In New Netherland, bakers used white bread in the lucrative trade with Native Americans. Frequent government ordinances attempted to curtail this trade to reserve enough flour to bake bread for the settlers. With no seventeenth-century recipes for bread available, the cookbook includes a modern recipe that explains how to shape the roll portrayed in the painting.   PGR

6 Abraham van Beyeren (c. 1620–1690)
Preparations for a Meal

Dutch, 1664

oil on canvas, 31¾ x 27 inches

signed and dated, upper right, with monogram: "AVB f 1664"

The Detroit Institute of Arts; Founders Society Purchase, 35.21

OYSTERS, some opened to reveal the glistening flesh of this prized bivalve and garnished with a few wedges of orange, are set on a table partially covered with a dark cloth. A brass mortar and pestle, a whole Seville orange, a redware pitcher with a pewter lid, a *façon de Venise* serpent-stemmed wine glass, partially filled with wine, and a plucked rooster with its dark wing feathers intact complete the table arrangement. The table fronts a wall relieved by an arched doorway. A bloody chunk of organ meats, liver, lungs, and heart, is suspended by an esophagus from a hook above the table, awaiting preparation.

Abraham van Beyeren's mastery in capturing texture is abundantly clear in this somewhat startling picture. The gleaming cool metallic lid on the pitcher and warm glow of the mortar and pestle contrast with the scaly stiff claws and scrawny plucked neck of the rooster, the laminated layers of the oyster shell, and the soft glistening flesh of the organ meats surrounded by their layers of fat. The organ meats grimly and cleverly mirror the plucked body and neck of the rooster. The orange tones of the animal parts, the redware jug, the cock's comb, and the citrus fruits are complemented by the yellow and gold tints of the mortar and pestle, nails on the fowl's claws, and the wine. These colors contrast sharply with the darker green hues of the closed oyster shell, orange leaf, and rumpled cloth.

Suspended entrails and offal were important elements in Pieter Aertsen's *Meat Pantry of an Inn, with the Virgin Giving Alms,* of 1551. No such religious element is found in this picture by Van Beyeren. Interestingly the same bird, organ meats, and mortar and pestle are combined with a dead rabbit and bunch of grapes in Van Beyeren's *Still Life with Game and Fowl* at Mauritshuis in The Hague.   DRB

THE MORTAR AND PESTLE stand ready to crush spices for the fowl and offal dishes to be prepared. Piquant orange zest and juice were probably added to accentuate the flavor. Surprisingly, *De Verstandige Kock* does not give any instructions on how to cook heart or lung. However, the preparations of tripe, cut in strips and rolled with rice and lean meat; head-meat pickled with vinegar and horseradish; and feet and muzzle, stewed with wine, butter, currants and crushed cloves, are extensively discussed in one of its appendixes, "De Hollantse Slacht-tijdt" (The Dutch butchering time).

De Verstandige Kock does give a recipe for "lemon heart," a heart-shaped, large meatball that might be more appealing to today's tastes. "Take minced veal just like for meatballs, add to it nutmeg, pepper and salt as well as peels of a fresh lemon cut into small pieces, for each pound of meat an egg yolk, a crushed rusk and mix it all together, shape it in the form of a large meatball or in the form of a heart, stew it with little water. When done take off the fat, add verjuice, butter, and peels of a salted lemon, which has been boiled in water first. Let it come to a boil together, then dish up; a sauce is poured over made from verjuice beaten with egg yolks." See cookbook for modern recipe.   PGR

7 Attributed to Abraham Bloemaert (1566–1651)
A Couple in a Kitchen Interior (The Prodigal Son)

Dutch, c. 1590–1600

oil on panel; 36½ x 51 inches

Private collection; courtesy of Lawrence Steigrad Fine Arts

A YOUNG MAN with whiskers and a ruddy complexion, wearing a feather-trimmed cap, sits close to a flirtatious kitchen maid dressed in a tight red bodice, her collar open in dishabille. An earthenware jug in his hand and an empty *berkemeier* wine glass confirm the man's swozzled state! While the maid uses one hand to finger his chest, the other lifts a coin from his wallet.

This bawdy kitchen scene is laden with foods which have erotic overtones. The dead duck on the table and hanging cockerel allude to "birding," a slang term for sexual intercourse. Broken eggshells and two eggs in testicular formation are echoed in the phallic shape of the sausages, in the hanging basket and the basket with the sheep's head near the young man.

A bunch of onions draped over the table's edge is a reminder of a well-known stimulus to eroticism. Viewers may also read the ham, bulbous earthenware jug, and ovoid pewter jug either as typical kitchen items or, like the hanging metal pot and earthenware pipkin, as allusions to a womb.

Among the seemingly innocent foods are pancakes, red and green cabbages, pig's feet, a roll, and a plate of herring on the table and cheeses ageing overhead in the rafters. Yet the male figure in the doorway, vomiting, gives strong indication that this is no ordinary kitchen scene but one where a prodigal son is squandering his father's money in drunkenness and gluttony, with the sin of fornication soon to follow.

Saint Luke's story "The Prodigal Son" (Luke 15:11–32) was popular in the Netherlands during the seventeenth century, perhaps because it provided a legitimate occasion for erotic art in staunch Calvinists' homes, carrying with it the promise of the father's forgiveness upon his son's return, much as Christ's crucifixion absolved humanity from original sin. A society in which so many people prospered at a heretofore unprecedented level of luxury needed reassurance that its members' new lifestyle did not preclude redemption. DRB

AN OVERWHELMING ARRAY of foodstuffs is waiting to be cooked while the maid is otherwise occupied. The rooster might be used in a raised pie and its cockscomb added to a stew; the duck will be stuffed with a dressing of grated bread, currants, cinnamon, sugar, and, according to *De Verstandige Kock*, "a good piece of butter." The onions will be used in a sauce. Only the pancakes are ready to eat. Pancakes were and are a favorite meal in the Netherlands, not for breakfast, but often for the main meal. Nowadays they come in a wide variety of flavors and fillings.

In the seventeenth century they were also sold on the street as snacks, as depicted in two other paintings in this book, (see cats. 41 and 50). Very few ingredients are required to make "common" pancakes: just mix one pound of flour with one pint of milk and three eggs. "Some add some Sugar," says the recipe. However, *De Verstandige Kock* also tells how to prepare "the best kind." "Take 5 or 6 eggs beaten with clean, running water, add to it cloves, cinnamon, mace and nutmeg with some salt, beat it with some wheat flour as thick as you like, fry them and sprinkle them with sugar; these are prepared with running water because [when prepared] with milk or cream they would be tough." See cookbook for modern recipe. PGR

42

8 Hendrick Bloemaert (1601–1672)
The Apple Seller (also known as Grocery Seller with Young Boy)

Dutch, c. 1623

oil on canvas; 28 x 23 inches

illegibly signed and dated on the face of the wooden tub: "HB f. 16-"

Milwaukee Art Museum; centennial gift of Dr. and Mrs. Alfred Bader, M1988.181

THE APPLE SELLER, a toothless old woman, her face a mass of wrinkles and her gnarled hands swollen with arthritis, is identified by the wooden tub of apples held under her arm. She faces a young boy, whose smooth complexion and dainty hands, marked by tiny fingernails, sharply contrast with hers. She points her index finger, in what may be an indecent gesture, toward one of her apples, encouraging the lad to select it.

The apple seller's head is wrapped in a white scarf, which calls further attention to her age and features: prominent cheekbones, sagging jaw, thin lips, and long nose. A loose-fitting collar encircles her throat. She is wearing a bright red jacket, typical of market sellers. The boy wears a lightly ruffed collar, whose folds are echoed in a bunch of young, tender leaves at the lower left. The dark green pole beans in the wicker basket provide another contrasting hue, as do the carrots in the background, and the blush of color on the apples is repeated on the boy's cheeks and ear.

Is the apple seller an incarnation of worldly experience and temptation juxtaposed with a youth who bespeaks Adamic innocence? Or has the artist merely allowed the viewer's eyes to appreciate his talent in capturing the nuances of young and old flesh and physiognomy? The shriveled faces of elderly women intrigued both Hendrick Bloemaert and his father, Abraham, who painted toothless old women at least four times between 1630 and 1635. However, toothlessness was not in itself disreputable; the exceedingly wealthy Margaretha de Geer, wife of the rich entrepreneur Jacob Trip, had her portrait painted by Nicolaes Maes late in life, and no attempt was made to disguise her lack of teeth. DRB

SEVERAL PAINTINGS in this book feature apples (see cats. 17, 27, 36, 44, 50, and 53). They were an important fruit to the Dutch, because apples kept well during the winter months and could also be dried. Today's cook does not have as large a variety to choose from as his or her seventeenth-century counterpart. Then, each kind had a specific use—for fritters, custards, or raised pies, for example—as the recipes in De Verstandige Kock indicate. Travelers to New Netherland commented on the excellent quality of the apples there. Jasper Danckaerts (1639–c. 1702), a Dutch Labadist, comments in his 1679–1680 journal that he had never seen "finer apples" (1913). He mentions specifically the Newtown Pippin, the Esopus Spitzenburgh, and the Poughkeepsie Swaar apple. Some of the old varieties are still grown in the orchards of the Hudson Valley. De Verstandige Kock lists four recipes for raised apple pies. The following recipe spices the double-crusted pastry with cinnamon and anise seed for an unusual, but very agreeable flavor. "Take apples, peel them and cut them in quarters and remove the cores, and then cut them in even smaller thin slivers, three quarter pound currants washed clean and three quarter pound sugar, a loot [14 grams] crushed cinnamon, then place the dough in the pan and first sprinkle apples into it, then currants, sugar, and cinnamon and pieces of butter. Repeat the layers until the pan is full; some add crushed anise seed. Then a lid of dough on top cut a hole in the lid here and there and let it bake with fire underneath and on top." A modern version of this recipe and another for the pole beans portrayed in a basket in the left corner, can be found in the cookbook. PGR

9 Pieter de Bloot (1601–1658)

Kitchen Table with Pumpkins, Cabbages, Onions, Artichokes, Meat, and Fruit

Dutch, 1636

oil on panel; 9⅞ x 11⅜ inches

signed and dated (left of lidded jar): "P. de Bloot 1636"

Private collection

ON A TABLE LAID with a red cloth, there is a large pumpkin, artichokes, some quince, an earthenware bowl of fruit, a string of onions, a basket overflowing with green and red cabbage, a curly-leaved Savoy cabbage, an earthenware plate of meat, and a round earthenware mug with a pewter lid. Raw meat is arranged on a wooden stand behind the table, near a brick wall.

Although the artist paid close attention to the various textures of all the produce, his detailed observations are especially noted on the opened leaves of the artichoke, papery skin of the onions, carefully woven wicker basket, and the cabbage leaves.

Pieter de Bloot created a number of still-life arrangements featuring cooking utensils and foods set in barns or rustic peasant interiors. His *Christ in the House of Martha and Mary* employed a religious theme, while incorporating such homely objects as a string of onions and cabbages in a wicker basket. Whether this picture is complete or cut down from a larger work with a religious theme is open to some dispute. If so, it would have provided another layer of meaning for viewers, instead of being just a beautiful evocation of the bounty provided by country gardens and the pleasures of rural life. Rustic settings for still-life arrangements of foods, baskets, and cooking utensils were persistently popular with several Rotterdam artists from the 1630s through the 1670s.

DRB

RECIPES FOR ARTICHOKES, red and green cabbages, onions, quince, and apples are included in *De Verstandige Kock*, and modern versions can be found in the cookbook. The meat trimmings in the basket at the left-hand corner of the painting were probably chopped and used for meatballs. Meatballs were apparently a popular dish, since there are five recipes for them in *De Verstandige Kock*. The fact that they can be made by finely chopping tough pieces of meat to turn them into soft tasty morsels no doubt added to their appeal in a time of rampant tooth decay. Recipes for meatballs are also frequently found in the cookbooks kept by descendants of the New Netherland settlers.

A recipe in *De Verstandige Kock* even suggests shaping a large meatball in the form of a heart (see cookbook and cat. 6). The following recipe from the same book is equally inventive; it tucks a cooked egg yolk in each meatball and wraps them in heads of tender, young Boston lettuce. "Take chopped veal with veal-fat a little fatter than usual and then spiced with nutmeg and a little mace, pepper and salt as appropriate, knead it together, take as many of the tender heads as you please and clean off the outer leaves and then washed clean and open up the inner leaves of the head, take then as many eggs as you have heads, make also as many little meatballs and place in the middle of each the yolk of an egg, put inside the head, tie with a string, and when the water boils put them in the pot, when it is done you could add to the broth a little finely crushed rusk and some butter, some gooseberries or unripe grapes or verjuice, according to everyone's liking." See cookbook for modern recipe.

PGR

10 Maerten Boelema, "de Stomme" (active 1640–1664)
Carved Ham, Silver Mustard Jar, and Glasses

Dutch, c. 1650s
oil on panel; 29⅞ x 23⅝ inches
Private collection

A WHITE LINEN CLOTH, smoothly arranged at left and bunched and loosely folded at right, dominates a table laden with large metal and glass serving pieces. A pewter platter holding a carved baked ham studded with cloves is positioned behind another pewter dish and carving knife placed precariously on the table. A prunted *roemer* filled with white wine, a roll, an octagonal *pasglas* (a clear cylindrical glass with dark-colored coils marking measures) holding beer, a silver mustard pot and spoon, and an overturned chased silver *tazza* complete the composition.

By virtue of its somber, monochromatic coloration and basic foodstuffs, this work would be called an *ontbijtje*. During the seventeenth century, estate inventories frequently listed such works as *hammetjes*, so popular was the theme of ham in pictures. Boelema was also capable of producing more elaborate luxury still lifes; a *pronk* still life by him features a nautilus cup, silver salt, and tall flute, along with other high-end elements.

Known as "de Stomme" (the mute), Boelema, a Friesland native, was a pupil of Willem Claesz. Heda in Haarlem, who may have influenced his choice of subject matter. Boelema certainly shared with many Haarlem painters, including Pieter Claesz. and Gerret Willem Heda (see cat. 23), an especial interest in the depiction of hams, *tazzas* and *pasglazen*. An overturned *tazza* gave the artist an opportunity to display foreshortening skills, creating a visual illusion.

The cloves in this ham cast a shadow on the fat, and perhaps made some viewers' mouths anticipate the spicy taste. For others, the cloves might symbolize the nails used during Christ's Crucifixion, as the Dutch word *nagel* is used both for cloves and nails. Viewers who preferred the religious import might have associated the bread roll and *roemer* of wine with the Eucharist.   DRB

AS THE LONG PROTRUDING BONE indicates, this rosy smoked ham with its thick layer of fat has been partially eaten. In November, the slaughter month, hams were prepared for smoking. They were first rubbed all over with salt and allowed to marinate or "pickle" for three days and three nights. "De Hollantse Slacht-tijdt" (The Dutch butchering time), the first appendix of *De Verstandige Kock*, suggests hanging hams in the chimney without covering, so that they were smoked through. By the middle of January, when they were cured, the hams were washed and dried outside for a day and hung from a beam in the kitchen until ready for use. The ham in this painting was studded with cloves and spit-roasted to heat through and to create the crackling crust. It is clear that New Netherland settlers tried to duplicate their life in the homeland, so it seems safe to assume that ham was as favorite a dish there as it was in the Netherlands. Pigs, cows, and horses were transported to the colony to provide meat, milk for butter and cheese, and transportation. A modern recipe on how to oven-roast a fresh ham can be found in the cookbook.   PGR

11 Jan de Bondt (?–1653)
Fish Market with Two Figures

Dutch, before 1653

oil on canvas; 48¼ x 58 inches

Wadsworth Atheneum Museum of Art; The Ella Gallup Sumner and Mary Catlin Sumner Collection Fund, 1943.53

A YOUNG WOMAN balancing a shallow earthenware dish containing a flounder and herring gives coins to an elderly fishmonger. His silvery hair and beard are echoed in the shiny bodies of the fish and in the white cap, ruff collar, and sleeves of his customer.

Most of the round-bodied fish have their mouths agape. The largest, a cod, placed prominently in the center, dwarfs the small herring. De Bondt, known for his fish still lifes, must have taken visual delight in capturing their sinuous, curving bodies and gleaming, seemingly alert eyes, all signs of a fresh catch.

He is known to have collaborated with Herman Saftleven (1609–1685), who would often supply the landscape background for his fish studies.

This market scene might reflect the prominence of fish in the Dutch daily diet or the economic significance of fish in Dutch trade. Since fish have a phallic suggestiveness, there might also be an erotic inference about the young woman and old man. Theologically minded viewers were probably reminded of Christ's disciples as "fishers of men." Connoisseurs still take delight in the artist's skillful use of a limited palette and "arabesque" or swerving lines. But regardless of the interpretation, this painting invites more than one viewing.

Fish markets, featuring sellers, buyers, and the all-important piscatorial product, were explored in the seventeenth century by many Dutch artists. The fish still life was a thematic emphasis in Dutch art (see cats. 22 and 36). Fish depicted in harbor settings constituted another typical theme for Jan van Kessel, the Elder, and Willem Ormea (see cat. 37).   DRB

COD HAS BEEN CALLED the most important food fish in the world. Caught in abundant quantities off Newfoundland as early as the 1400s and along the Norwegian coast several hundred years before that, cod has been so overfished that today's numbers have seriously dwindled. In the seventeenth century, however, cod was plentiful. It was served fresh, or preserved by drying and salting. Dried cod was a standard part of the victuals on Dutch war and trading ships. It keeps indefinitely and can be rehydrated as needed.

Adriaen van der Donck of New Netherland reported that "Outside at sea, and in some of the bays of the East river, the codfish are very plenty." He thought that experienced Dutch fishermen easily "could take ship loads of codfish" (1968). They must have done so, because we know that fifteen hundred pounds of dried cod were used as provisions in a 1655 military campaign when Petrus Stuyvesant (c. 1610–1672), the director of the colony, invaded New Sweden (now Delaware).

De Verstandige Kock has only one recipe for fresh cod. "Take the thick slices of fish, place them in a tin platter not quite covered with water, sprinkle some crushed pepper over it and whole mace, a little salt, and some crushed rusk, and do add butter. Let it stew together about an hour and a half with fire under it and above, then add a fresh lemon or lemon juice. It is quite easy to eat." See cookbook for modern recipe.   PGR

12 Gerard ter Borch (1617–1681)
Woman Pouring Wine

Dutch, c. 1650

oil on panel; 13^{15}/$_{16}$ x 10^{7}/$_{8}$ inches

Brooklyn Museum of Art; gift of the executors of Colonel Michael Friedsam, 34.494

AN ATTRACTIVE *meisje* (girl or young woman), with light brown hair worn in a bun and covered with a modest black cap, dressed in a brilliant red jacket over a white cambric blouse, is seated near an older man who is filling his pipe with tobacco. She is pouring wine from a silver ewer into a stemmed goblet. Her eyes are focused on the task at hand. Her lips are slightly parted in speech. An elderly woman seated behind this couple is garbed in dark clothing with a white collar and headscarf. She holds a silver tray. No expression plays across her broad face, her lips are sealed and eyes downcast so as to appear closed.

Gerard ter Borch probably used his sister, Gesina, as the model for the girl, as she appears in a number of his pictures. With a delicate touch, he has managed to capture the red piping on the sleeves and shoulders of her garment and the multiple folds in her skirt. He has also managed to create a scene of considerable ambiguity. Is this a simple domestic picture featuring a sister pouring wine for her older brother? Or might this be read as an erotic encounter with a young prostitute, in the company of her procuress (madam), pouring a drink for a client? His finger, thrust into the pipe bowl, would be read by many of Ter Borch's contemporaries as an allusion to sexual intercourse.

Certainly Ter Borch returned to the theme of love for sale in a number of pictures, including his *Parental Admonition*, *The Gallant Officer*, *Soldier Offering a Young Woman Coins*, and *Young Couple Drinking Wine*. Wine is often associated with seduction, and the theme of the procuress and whore occurs in many Dutch paintings, some as subtle as this and others more clearly identifiable as bordello scenes (see cat. 42).

DRB

SWEETER, LESS PERISHABLE WINES from the Mediterranean were popular with the wealthy, but according to *De Verstandige Kock* should not be used for cooking, because they turned bitter when heated. Instead, Rhine and Mosel wines were suggested, which then were sour (dry), not sweet. Wines were exported to New Netherland as trade goods. Apparently shipping wine was often troublesome. Jeremias van Rensselaer (1632–1674), the third patroon of Rensselaerswijck, sent many letters to the homeland reporting on casks that had leaked or wine that had turned. Now and then he remarked on a wine of excellent quality that is "too good to be drunk in taverns" (1932).

In upper-class households, the sour wines, red or white, were made into spiced mulled wine called hippocras. This was served traditionally with wafers as a dessert course, reminiscent of the communion ceremony. In medieval times Hippocras and wafers were reserved for the nobility. Gradually the upper classes took them up. When sugar became more available, wafers were replaced by sweetmeats. Although hippocras at first accompanied the new showy dessert course, it later became the ceremonial drink at Dutch weddings, and then was referred to as "bride's tears."

A modern version of Hippocras, adapted from a variety of sources, can be found in the cookbook accompanying this volume, together with a recipe for wafers from *De Verstandige Kock*. The latter reads: "Take a pound wheat flour, a loot [14 grams] cinnamon, a half loot ginger, 2 eggs, a half beer glass Rhenish wine, a stuyver [five cents' worth] rosewater, a small bowl butter with salt, a little sugar; beaten with some lukewarm water until the thickness of pancake [batter] and fried in the iron. Is delicious."

PGR

13 Pieter van den Bosch (c. 1613–1663)

An Artist in His Studio

Dutch, c. 1650s

oil on wood panel; 21¼ x 28 inches

University of Virginia Art Museum; museum purchase with funds from the Volunteer Board Endowment Fund and the Curriculum Support Fund, 1994.2

IN A STUDIO SETTING, an artist, holding a palette loaded with pigments, paintbrushes, and a maulstick, gazes at an arrangement of rustic kitchen utensils and vegetables placed on the floor. A canvas, laced with cord onto a wooden frame, is positioned on the easel before him. His still-life models include a huge pumpkin, a large leafy cabbage, wooden tubs, and a white stoneware pitcher.

The artist seems too dressed-up to paint. His fashionable black doublet features gold buttons and a silver trimmed sash, and his dun-colored mantle is fur-trimmed. A sheathed sword with an ornate handle and a dark cape trimmed with gold braid hang behind him.

Although the viewer is unable to "see" the painting on the canvas, the contrived grouping of foods and household objects suggests he is working on a still life set in a peasant barn interior. It is impossible to tell at what stage the artist is, but the pristine nature of his attire and surroundings suggests a beginning. The placement of this arrangement is from the viewer's perspective, not the painter's; his vantage point actually could not have given him a good view of the objects. The painter's status imputes social importance to his art even though the most commonplace foods and utensils are his subjects.

Artists' workshops are depicted in many seventeenth-century Dutch and Flemish paintings, drawings, and prints. Studio activities such as grinding pigment, drawing from models, painting still lifes or posed sitters, laying out colors, or using a maulstick are highlighted. Occasionally the artist is seen working in the company of art connoisseurs and patrons, or teaching an apprentice.

Elegantly dressed painters are often depicted in their studios playing musical instruments. The association of painting with music or literature is a theme in many seventeenth-century Dutch paintings, especially the work of the Delft master Johannes Vermeer (1632–1675). Bosch's young artist, however, is more the confident cavalier. DRB

THE LARGE-HEADED CABBAGE is often referred to as Leiden cabbage, presumably, because it originated in or around that Dutch city. No doubt this was the "large headed cabbage" that Jeremias van Rensselaer (1632–1674) had in mind when he ordered cabbage seed to be sent from the Netherlands (1932). De Verstandige Kock mentions cabbage in salads and contains a recipe for Savoy cabbage and for cauliflower (see cat. 36 and cookbook for a modern version). The Dutch called the other vegetable portrayed *pompoen* (pumpkin). Part of the problem in determining the origin of melons, gourds, pumpkins, and squash stems from the confusion of their names in early texts. With their interesting shapes and beautiful color variation, gourds might have resembled pumpkins. Often cultivated for ornamental use, some varieties can be eaten, which adds to the confusion. In spite of an ongoing debate, it seems reasonable to say that melon and gourds were Old World plants, while pumpkins and squash were New World plants, unknown in Europe before the explorations of Columbus.

In New Netherland, the Dutch, English, and Swedish colonists planted great quantities of oblong pumpkins. Indicative of the identification problem, Swedish botanist Peter Kalm thought that pumpkins came to America from Europe. Settlers would cut them in half and boil them or roast them in front of the fire. On both sides of the Atlantic, the Dutch added their own twist and boiled them twice, the second time with milk, to make a kind of porridge. PGR

14 Salomon de Bray (1597–1664)
Child with Cherries

Dutch, c. 1655
oil on panel; 23 x 18½ inches
Memorial Art Gallery of the University of Rochester; Bertha Buswell Bequest, 55.65

A BLONDE-HAIRED BOY, the picture of good health and affluence, grips a wicker basket filled with ripe red cherries. Pink cheeks, plump, rosy lips, and red flowers on the child's shawl echo the cerise hue. All evoke thoughts of early summer, childhood's simple joys, and innocence.

The rosy tones contrast with the deep green used on the child's jacket, sash, and on the stems and leaves of the cherries. The golden tones of his hair also appear on the wicker basket and thread of gold silk woven into the sash. The boy's hazel eyes look out calmly at the viewer, engaging contact and provoking thought. Did the painter mean to suggest that sensual pleasures and childhood are both as delicious and as fleeting as fresh-picked cherries? Or does the presence of the child suggest parental nurturing and attention to his temporal and spiritual needs in the same way that a gardener cultivates cherry orchards? Did viewers imagine the boy's upbringing that of taming wild undisciplined nature? Or did they see the portrait as proof of parental fruitfulness, pride, and affection?

Although the Memorial Art Gallery attributes this unsigned picture to Salomon de Bray, stylistically it closely resembles one by his son. Jan de Bray's portrait of an older blonde boy, Portrait of a Boy Holding a Basket of Fruit, is signed and dated 1658 (Museum of Fine Arts, Boston). DRB

CHERRIES WERE a popular fruit in both the Netherlands and New Netherland, where orchards were established early on. In 1639, Anthony Jansz. van Salee sold a house to Barent Dircksz. The record of the sale mentions an orchard behind it containing no fewer than seventy-three cherry trees, as well as apple and peach trees and grape vines. No doubt those cherries were sold locally and preserved for winter. In "De Verstandige Confituur-maker" (The sensible confectioner), an appendix to De Verstandige Kock instructing readers "how good and useful preserves can be made from all sorts of fruits," five recipes are listed for cherries.

For the charming little boy depicted in the portrait, a recipe for cherry fruit leather from this appendix, still a favorite treat for children, is added to the cookbook. As we can see in Osias Beert's painting (see cat. 2) it could also be made from quinces. Prepared without sugar and dried in the sun, fruit leather was a popular and inexpensive way of preserving all kinds of fruit. "Take Cherries that are somewhat sour, take off the stems, boil them in an earthenware pot without liquid on a low fire, when they start to cook in their own juice stir them so that they do not burn, they are done when the outer skin comes off and the meat has become a thick porridge; let them cool and rub them through a turned-over Sieve, take the resulting porridge and spread it on glazed tiles, let it dry this way in the sun or in an oven when the bread has been removed, take it from the dish and save it." See cookbook for modern recipe. PGR

15 Quiringh Gerritsz. van Brekelenkam (c. 1620–c. 1668)
Old Woman Scraping Carrots (also known as Old Woman Sitting at Her Fireplace)

Dutch, c. 1655

oil on panel; 11½ x 14½ inches

New Orleans Museum of Art; gift of Allen H. Johness, Jr., 76.306

AN ELDERLY WOMAN, seated by the fireplace, is scraping carrots. On the floor a bunch of white carrots awaits preparation. A covered redware pot rests on the hearth, where the carrots will be mixed with the stew. The tongs near the fireplace will be used to position coals and the wooden sticks will provide cooking fuel. The setting is modest but neat. The bed curtains are parted to reveal linen-covered pillows. The doors of the cupboard are shut tight, and a blue-and-white Westerwald jug rests atop it. A marine painting hangs on the wall. Dutch artists often included pictures or maps to decorate household interiors. Although Brekelenkam incorporated landscapes in many pictures, he was not known for his seascapes, indicating that this subject held special significance for him or his patron.

The subject is a respectable gentlewoman, as demonstrated by her covered hair and the prominently placed spinning wheel. Spinning remained a symbol of domestic virtue for women, even when most Dutch women no longer spun at home, but purchased threads and cloth from fabric shops. The spinning wheel functioned as a *topos* (a conventional symbol or visual metaphor) in seventeenth-century Dutch art, reminding viewers of *Proverbs 31*, which praised a woman who spun as virtuous.

Some viewers might interpret the shoe on the floor as a symbol of her faithfulness and steadfastness, or surmise that her husband was lost at sea, his memory evoked in the marine painting. Others might appreciate the black mule as a counterpoint to the black frame, dark bed curtains, and woman's costume. These somber colors contrast with the warm brown-toned wooden objects and the reddish hues of the hearth, the pot, and the woman's sleeves.

Brekelenkam had a penchant for women engaged in household tasks. He often painted them in kitchen settings and frequently emphasized women's roles as mothers (see cat. 17). DRB

WHITE, YELLOW, and red carrots were available in the seventeenth century. Orange carrots, so popular today, were developed from the yellow and red types, probably in the Dutch City of Hoorn, because they were often referred to as "Hoorn carrots." Together with turnips and parsnips, carrots were the root vegetables most frequently eaten, either as side dishes or in stews. Large-scale horticultural experimentation for commercial purposes and private pleasure took place at this time in the Leiden and Amsterdam botanical gardens and in the gardens of the country houses owned by the wealthy upper classes.

In New Netherland, as in the homeland, carrots and parsnips were part of the kitchen garden. Vegetables flourished and required less care and attention in the fertile new colony, called "a land of milk and honey" by Jacob Steendam, one of its early poets (Murphy 1861). *De Verstandige Kock* gives no recipe for carrots, but two for parsnips. Carrots and parsnips cooked together look pretty and have complementary flavors. A handful of parsley finishes the dish. A modern recipe suitable for fireplace cooking can be found in the cookbook. PGR

16 Quiringh Gerritsz. van Brekelenkam (c. 1620–c. 1668)
Old Man Scaling Fish

Dutch, early 1660s

oil on panel; 16½ x 21½ inches

Van Cortlandt House Museum; The National Society of Colonial Dames in the State of New York, Photograph by John Maggiotto

AN ELDERLY MAN, his beard and mustache white with age, sits indoors, scaling small fish on a cutting board arranged across his knees. On the floor near his feet is a wooden tub filled with water and small live fish. Scaled fish are draining in an earthenware colander.

Light streams in from the half-opened doorway to illuminate the old man's task. Leafy trees in a country setting indicate that this is a rustic cottage. The old man is dressed, peasant style, in a soft dark cap, sturdy light-colored coat, dark breeches, and hose. A beer barrel serves as his tabletop; an earthenware mug sits atop it; and a broom rests against the rim.

Scattered on the floor are mussel shells, a wooden ladle, a blue-and-white Dutch majolica dish with an overturned earthenware cooking pot on top of it, and an iron kettle lined with brass and edged with copper. The kitchen door is open at right, giving a view of his wife cooking at a fireplace. This serene scene presents a nice division of labor: he prepares the fish, and she cooks them. No doubt they have performed these simple tasks many times in their years together. The spinning wheel in the front room alludes to her domestic virtue.

Brekelenkam found a clientele for quiet scenes of domestic life. Affluent Leiden residents—university professors, merchants, lawyers, physicians, and woolen cloth manufacturers—must have enjoyed representations of lives presumed to be simpler than theirs. Certainly a married woman living on the Rapenburg—Leiden's most prestigious address—would be mildly amused at the haphazard array of cooking utensils on the floor. No mussel shells would litter her scrubbed and polished marble floors! And her husband would not sully his fingers with the scales of fish.   DRB

IT IS IMPOSSIBLE to discern what kind of little fish the old man is readying for a meal. He might even be cleaning a large batch to cook and sell at one of the stalls offering prepared fish, located on the outskirts of the fish markets. The fish could very well be smelt, which was fried, either rolled in flour or without coating, in very hot oil until done. Gheeraert Vorselman, in *Een Nyeuwen Coock Boeck*, published in the middle of the sixteenth century, suggested that smelt and other fried fish be served with a sauce. Made from almonds, bread, saffron, and garlic mashed together in a mortar and pestle, this mixture is cooked in wine long enough for the flavors to mingle. A sauce with these expensive ingredients would be well beyond the means of this man in his modest house. He would have eaten his fried fish with a little sauce of vinegar and butter.   PGR

17 Quiringh Gerritsz. van Brekelenkam (c. 1620 – c. 1668)
Mother and Child in an Interior

Dutch, c. 1660

oil on panel; 27⅛ x 18⅝ inches

Allen Memorial Art Museum, Oberlin College, Oberlin, Ohio; gift of Dr. Alfred R. Bader, Parks Campbell, Robert M. Light, and Ruth C. Roush, in honor of Professor Wolfgang Stechow, 1972.47

AN AFFLUENT MOTHER holds up an apple for her chubby-faced child, who is seated in a *kinderstoel* (infant's high chair), reaching a tiny hand toward the fruit. The mother's shoes on the floor indicate that she is staying at home to carry out maternal responsibilities.

Her feet remain hidden under a rose-colored skirt and voluminous apron topped by a dark overdress edged with fur. A blouse, large collar, and headscarf complete her attire. The heavy clothing and blazing fire suggest that this is a cold, wintry day.

The child is dressed in an embroidered cap edged with lace and a bib collar worn over a red gown. Since boys and girls were dressed alike at this age, it is impossible to determine the child's gender. On the baby's tray a rod with movable balls has been attached for amusement. Like an abacus, this plaything will eventually help the child learn to count. The carved back of the high chair supports the child just as the tabletop protectively encloses the youngster. A gray cat warms itself on the hearth. Above the fireplace, a mantel holds three majolica dishes.

This painting is comparable to many of Brekelenkam's pictures of domestic life dating to the 1650s and 1660s. The warm brown, ochre, gray, black, red, and white pigments are his usual palette. The soft contours of the faces and strongly modeled folds in her apron are typical of his style. The details on the *kinderstoel* reflect his painterly attention to furnishings found in both modest and middle-class households.

Brekelenkam created many pictures of women with children. His women slice bread, rock cradles, wash dishes, make lace, spoon-feed infants, and make pancakes for the family. In short, they perform the everyday domestic tasks that were thought essential to fulfilling their roles as mothers and housewives. This picture also points to another important maternal responsibility. The child is reaching for an apple, the symbol of knowledge, indicating that the mother must teach not only the word *appel*, but also which other food items are edible and nutritious. In addition, she will instruct her child in the importance of knowledge, especially good moral conduct. DRB

THE APPLE the mother holds in her hand might become a part of a Shoemaker's *Taert*, a raised pie made from pureed apples cooked in their own juices and layered with bread crumbs, a recipe that still appears in Dutch cookbooks. The *taert* is soft, yet holds together. It would be easy to eat and a wonderful treat for the little darling in the beautiful chair.

De Verstandige Kock has the following recipe: "Take sour apples, peel them and cut them in pieces and when they have been cooked until done mash them fine, then take butter, sugar and currants, everyone according to his taste, and stir that together with 4 or 5 eggs, then take grated wheat bread and place that on the bottom of a platter, place your apples on top and again grate wheat bread on top [of the apples], cover it with a lid from a Taert-pan place fire on it. It makes a good crust." See cookbook for modern recipe. PGR

18 Quiringh Gerritsz. van Brekelenkam (c. 1620–c. 1668)
Vegetable Stall

Dutch, 1665

oil on panel; 18⅜ x 14⅞ inches

signed and dated bottom left: "Quierijn f. 1665"

The Detroit Institute of Arts; gift of James E. Scripps, 89.32

A CAREFREE, well-dressed young woman, carrying a metal shopping pail filled with a leafy green lettuce and a few onions, stands in front of an outdoor market stall. Daringly displaying a peek of her rose colored stocking, she ignores the gentleman behind her while nonchalantly sniffing a delicate pink flower. Brekelenkam used the same young woman in his 1663 picture, A Housewife and Maid with a Fish (present location unknown).

The elderly market woman, wearing pince nez, counts her coins. The plump vendor is seated behind her display table, which is covered with cucumbers and huge cabbages attractively framed with carrots arranged like the sun's rays. A wicker basket filled with more produce sits by her elbow. In front of the display table is a wooden bench with a plate of Kirby cucumbers. Another large cabbage and a cucumber are on the ground beneath the bench. While contemporary viewers might have understood the bartering and banter occurring between buyer and seller, they probably also marveled at the bravura display of carrots.

Brekelenkam depicted old women wearing or holding pince nez in several other paintings, especially when the subjects are reading the Bible or examining a child's hair for lice. Dutch scientific interest in optics, exemplified by Antony van Leeuwenhoek's work on the microscope, was paralleled by a growing popular use of eyeglasses, especially by the elderly.

Brekelenkam painted at least five other pictures of women fruit and vegetable vendors and four images of female fishmongers. Market women were a favorite theme not only for him but also for his artistic predecessors (see cats. 1, 8, and 44) and contemporaries (see cat. 59).   DRB

THE WOMAN carrying a pail of salad stuffs might have stopped at this vegetable stall to round out her selection with some of what we now call Kirby cucumbers, shown in the foreground. Salads, eaten at the beginning of the meal in both the Netherlands and New Netherland, consisted of a variety of greens, cucumbers, and herbs. Cucumbers were often cut ahead of time then sprinkled with salt and set aside. They were drained before being added to the salad. Cucumbers were also marinated in vinegar with pepper and horseradish to make pickles.

In New Netherland, a garden was planted as soon as a house was built. It would contain various salad greens, both medicinal and culinary herbs, and a large variety of vegetables. Settlers brought seeds for such gardens with them, but seeds were also sent from the homeland on Dutch trading vessels. The Dutch preferred a dressing of oil and vinegar, or melted butter and vinegar. Apparently a high proportion of vinegar to oil was used in New Netherland; Swedish botanist Peter Kalm, who visited the colony in the mid-eighteenth century, remarked with obvious disapproval that Dutch dressings were very sour (1987). Dutch physician Stephanus Blankaart, in his Borgerlijke Tafel (Bourgeois table) of 1633, likewise disapproved. He advised against the use of vinegar in salad dressings, preferring instead a little oil and salt, and encouraged the use of fresh herbs. The recipe in De Verstandige Kock gives a clear impression of the variety of greens grown in the country house gardens of affluent Dutch of the time. It lists head, leaf, and lamb's lettuce, dandelion shoots, endive, and many other salad stuffs, including cucumbers, a variety of herbs, and edible flowers. See cookbook.   PGR

19 Pieter Claesz. (c. 1597–c. 1661)
Still Life with Roemer, Shrimp, and Roll

Dutch, 1646

oil on panel; 15½ x 21¾ inches

signed and dated, left side, center (near glass): "P C" in monogram, "1646"

Isabel and Alfred Bader

THIS STILL LIFE of cooked shrimp in a blue and white Chinese bowl set atop a table covered with a pressed cloth features several elements found in other *ontbijtje* pictures by Pieter Claesz. The *roemer* of wine, crusty roll on a pewter dish, currant branch, and ebony knife handle projecting over the table's edge occur in many of his paintings. Claesz. included some ripe currants at left and a twist of paper filled with peppercorns at right.

The artist has effectively used curving lines and ovals, notably on the prunts of the goblet, the swell of the roll, the circular serving dishes, and the round fruits and olives. Even the shrimp curve in their shells. Light from the left is reflected on the glass, the wine, the pewter, the tablecloth, and the ivory inlay of the knife handle. This is a quiet, tranquil picture that illustrates the masterful use of a limited palette of colors. Created midway in Claesz.'s career, it has been called a work of his mature genius.

Along with fellow Haarlem artist Willem Claesz. Heda, Claesz. was an important innovator of the *ontbijtje*. These pictures often celebrated the simple foods and drink of everyday life in muted, subtle tones. He must have enjoyed using similar colors to capture different textures, as demonstrated here in the whites and pinks of the roll's crumb, the starched and pressed linen, the glazed porcelain, and the crumpled paper.

Contemporary viewers may have admired the modest elegance of this composition or interpreted the black and white knife handle as a symbol of good and evil. Claesz. frequently placed knives diagonally in his pictures; their often ornate handles suggest luxury amidst simple food items.

Numerous Dutch painters delighted in capturing the shapes and texture of *roemers*, which were ubiquitous in the Netherlands. Inexpensive drinking glasses imported from Germany or produced domestically, *roemers* were often featured in both simple *ontbijtje* and elaborate *banketje* still lifes.

DRB

AN APPETIZING DISH of shrimp and a white roll are waiting to be enjoyed with a *roemer* of wine. Shrimp were eaten—as the painting hints—as a snack rather than a meal. Recipes for shrimp are rare. They were mainly boiled in seawater and consumed on the spot by the fishermen or taken to market immediately. Mid-sixteenth-century author Gheeraert Vorselman alluded to the sea when he lyrically explained in his 1560 cookbook how to prepare shrimp. "Take lively shrimp; salt the water and allow it to come to a rolling boil, add some vinegar to the water, and throw in the shrimp, make sure they boil as if it were a sea and allow the waves to pass over them three or four times. Remove them to a colander and sprinkle with salt, is good to eat cold, peeled, with vinegar, pepper and chopped parsley" (1971). This recipe needs no modern adaptation.

PGR

20   Adriaen Coorte (c. 1660–after 1723)
Wild Strawberries on a Ledge

Dutch, 1704

oil on paper, laid down on panel; 5⅛ x 6¼ inches

signed and dated (lower left on stone ledge): "A Coorte/ 1704"

The Henry H. Weldon Collection

A GENEROUS HANDFUL of wild strawberries have been heaped on a chipped stone ledge. Most of the tiny berries are ripe, their red flesh revealing all the seeds on the prickly outer surfaces. These strawberries are known as *maandbloeyers* in the Netherlands, meaning that they bloom for a whole month. Some pictured here are still unripe, their yellow and green colors reflecting immaturity. A strawberry sprig bearing one perfect white flower with its characteristic five petals has been placed amongst the fruit. Two blossom ends of leaves are depicted with the sprig, one with the strawberry already plucked and the second with a very tiny immature berry. Two of the berries in the pile are still attached to their stems and leaves.

Viewers might have felt their mouths watering at the sight of these delicious, fragrant morsels. Perhaps some thought of summer pleasures, while others marveled at how tenderly the artist focused his attention and skill on this modest composition.

This is a tiny picture, a jewel like the garnet-toned fruit. Coorte, who signed and dated the picture on the left edge of the ledge, is known to have used strawberries in 20 percent of his recorded paintings. Whether he did so because of personal fondness for the fruit, because there was a clientele for such imagery in Middelburg, where he worked, or because strawberries created pictorial challenges for him remains a mystery.

Coorte's use of ledge compositions probably derived from still-life works by Balthasar van der Ast (c. 1593–1657) and by Ambrosius Bosschaert, the Elder (1573–1621), who worked in Middelburg many years prior to Coorte's career. Many Dutch artists arranged fruits, vegetables, flower vases, or shells on stone plinths or wooden ledges when creating still-life paintings. Others elected to use tabletops, stable floors, forest paths, or beach dunes as the base on which to arrange objects for carefully contrived depictions.   DRB

WILD STRAWBERRIES grew in fields and meadows, while cultivated strawberries were grown in orchards between and under the trees. Yet compared with today's varieties, early cultivated strawberries were very close to their wild predecessors. They had a long growing season and were fragrant and full of flavor. Strawberries were packaged in glazed earthenware cups with drainage holes and sold commercially. About thirty of these cups were layered in one basket and usually transported by boat to market. As a seasonal specialty, strawberries were eaten in a buttered *zottinnekoeck* (see cat. 40). In wealthy households they were also consumed lightly sugared, with French wine as accompaniment.

The early settlers of New Netherland and New England often commented on the abundance of wild strawberries there. By the eighteenth century, strawberry picking had become a social event for Dutch American youths. They would go into the hills, carrying a bottle of cream in their picnic baskets, to enjoy the fruit al fresco. A Scottish woman observing the custom in the 1760s marveled that young people were allowed to go out and about freely and unchaperoned.

De Verstandige Kock includes a pastry recipe that can be used for cherries, strawberries, gooseberries, currants, plums, and other soft fruits. "Take the most beautiful cherries [or strawberries] and when you have made the crust sprinkle enough sugar on the bottom to cover it, place a layer of cherries [strawberries] on it and then again a layer of sugar until the crust is filled, not forgetting cinnamon, cover it and let it bake until done." See cookbook for modern recipe.   PGR

21 Adriaen Coorte (c. 1660–after 1723)
Chestnuts on a Ledge

Dutch, 1705

oil on paper, laid down on panel; 5¼ x 6⅛ inches

signed and dated (on left edge of ledge): "ACoorte/ 1705"

The Henry H. Weldon Collection

FOUR CHESTNUTS have been arranged on a stone ledge, the brown shells cracked to reveal the golden brown nutmeats inside. Like his *Wild Strawberries on a Ledge* (see cat. 20), the artist signed and dated this small picture on the ledge, at the left side of the crack. Coorte's penchant for providing small, finely detailed, portraits of food items is revealed not only in diminutive nuts and berries, but in pictures where weightier produce, like bunches of asparagus, peaches, and cabbages, are featured. This is not his only rendition of chestnuts; in 1703 he painted *Five Chestnuts* and a picture known as *Chestnuts* as a pendant to his *Cherries*.

Whether chestnuts had any allegorical significance for Coorte is hard to say. He might have seen the chestnut as a symbol for the human heart, which some believe must have a shell to protect its owner's feelings.

Alternatively, Coorte may have regarded these chestnuts as marvels of nature—maybe even a manifestation of God's handiwork and bounty. For many of Coorte's contemporaries, the appearance of chestnuts in the marketplace marked the season of autumn, a harbinger of the winter yet to come. Perhaps the artist alludes to the changing seasons? No doubt many perceivers were primarily intrigued with the artist's talent in capturing the chestnuts in such a lifelike manner from different vantage points, inviting them to look closely, just as Coorte did. DRB

SWEET MEALY CHESTNUTS were boiled and served as a starch, the way potatoes are now eaten. Nobleman Floris II van Pallant ate them this way, served with turnips and fish, when he studied at Leiden University in the early seventeenth century. According to *De Verstandige Kock*, chestnuts were also used in a sumptuous *olipodrigo*, an elaborate stew that incorporated capon, lamb, veal, beef, sausages, pig's and sheep's feet, pork, marrowbones, veal meatballs, sweetbreads, and ram's testicles. Vegetables such as asparagus and artichokes in the spring or chestnuts in the fall were added as available. The dish was finished with a buttery egg sauce and served on a deep platter with a rim, which was rubbed with butter and sprinkled with a mixture of chopped hardboiled egg yolks, rusk crumbs, and crushed parsley. The recipe ends by saying: "is good."

Chestnut trees also grew in New Netherland, where Native Americans used the bark to cover their houses. In order to harvest the chestnuts, it was their habit to cut down the entire tree to remove the limbs. Although this practice reduced the number of trees, it also cleared the forest to create gardens for agriculture. Moreover, nut wood was preferred for cooking fires (see cat. 27). The cookbook includes a simple recipe for boiled chestnuts, incorporating Gheeraert Vorselman's suggestion, from his *Een Nyeuwen Coock Boeck* of 1560, to pour some melted butter over them and sprinkle the dish with sugar and cinnamon. PGR

22 Jacob Gillig (c. 1626–1701)
A Still Life of River Fish

Dutch, 1675

oil on panel; 15 x 7⅞ inches

signed and dated (at right above ledge): "J Gillig fecit A 1675"

Private collection

SEVEN FRESHWATER FISH represent the angler's catch; four are strung up through their gaping mouths. The fishing rod, bob, and wooden bait box suspended from a nail in the brick wall celebrate the fisherman's success. A burlap cloth cascading over the stone ledge will be used to carry the fish home. The shimmering scales, water droplets, and the gleaming, melancholy eyes of the dead fish attest to their freshness.

Gillig's pyramidal composition is masterful, as is his spare palette of colors. The gold and brown speckled bodies, dark stripes, and white underbellies glow. The warm brown tones of the tackle contrast nicely with the cooler dark ledge and shadows on the wall. The reddish threads in the burlap are echoed in fish fins and gills.

Freshwater fish still lifes were Jacob Gillig's specialty, whether he was depicting gutted fish prepared for cooking, or tackle, bait, and the catch.

Gillig's fishing rod and triangular arrangement of fish are also found in two more elaborate still lifes by Abraham Mignon, the Frankfurt-born painter who was working in Utrecht by 1669. Mignon was married to Gillig's wife's niece, suggesting the possibility of mutual inspiration.

Gillig worked for a while as a jailer in Utrecht, where the jail was located next to the fish market. Whether he was inspired by this contact, by Abraham Mignon's pictures, by the fish still lifes of his father-in-law, Abraham Willaert, or by those of his own teacher, Willem Ormea (see cat. 37), is unclear. In any case, his fascination for river fish is abundantly evident.   DRB

FRESHWATER FISH like perch, bass, or bream were used in a typical dish of the seventeenth and eighteenth centuries known as *doopvis* (fish for dunking). The freshly caught fish were cooked in salted water to which parsley was added. The cooking broth was then used for dunking the fish and bread that was served with it. It was a favorite meal at taverns and at *trekschuit* (canal boat) stops.

De Verstandige Kock contains eight recipes for freshwater fish. In one recipe, bream is stuffed with a dressing of its own roe, chopped egg yolks, parsley, and spices and roasted on a spit. Other recipes give directions for stewing carp in its own blood in the "high German manner," with wine, vinegar, and onion; preparing eel either stewed with green herbs like sorrel, chervil, and parsley, or cut in pieces and braised with butter, ginger, and onion; and boiling pike or carp "until blue." There are also three other recipes for pike, one of which follows (see cat. 59): "Take a pike cooked in water with some vinegar and salted appropriately, then cut bacon in cubes and fry it in butter until it is red [reddish brown], place it in a pot, add to it some broth, Rhenish wine, vinegar, mace, pepper, and ginger. Let it boil until properly thickened, place the pike in that [sauce] and dish up this way." See cookbook for modern recipe.   PGR

23 Gerret Willemsz. Heda (c. 1620–1702?)
Still Life with Ham

Dutch, 1650

oil on oak panel; 38½ x 32½ inches

signed and dated (lower right edge of white tablecloth): "HEDA 1650"

National Gallery of Art, Washington; gift of John S. Thacher, 1985.16.1

A TABLE COVERED with a dark cloth trimmed with gold fringe is painted against a warm ochre background. A crumpled white linen napkin is on the left side of the table. A pewter plate supports two prunted *berkemeiers*, partially filled with white wine. A metal platter bears a luscious smoked ham with its roasted skin rolled back to reveal pink flesh and succulent white fat. Knife cuts in the meat make it clear that slices have been carved from the bone. A knife with a ball-shaped ornamentation on its handle projects out over the table. Next to the knife sits a crusty roll.

A tall *façon de Venise* winged flute contains an ounce of white wine at the bottom. A pewter wine jug, its hinged lid open, stands next to the flute. A waffle-glass beaker, partially filled with amber beer, an ornate silver salt, trimmed on the top with three sculpted tulips, two silver plates, one atop the other, and an overturned silver mustard pot with a spoon complete the array.

Those familiar with paintings by Heda's father, Willem, would note his monochromatic tradition continuing in the son's work. Did Gerret Heda want his viewers to admire his skill in capturing the textures of fabrics, gleaming metals, sparkling glasses and liquid contents, the carved ham, the crunch and warm color of the roll's crust, and the granular white salt? Perhaps so, but he probably would have expected some viewers to interpret the partially drained glasses as a sign of moderation. The salt and mustard might suggest that one savor food items—and life—while time permitted. On the other hand, those who had made or lost fortunes during the speculative period of "tulip mania" in the 1630s might have interpreted the standing salt as a chastening reminder of the need for prudence in the face of folly. And no doubt those inclined to Christian interpretations would find hints of Holy Communion in the bread and wine.   DRB

Cierlijcke Voorsnijdinge Aller Tafelgerechten (Graceful carving [instructions] for all table dishes), an etiquette book on carving and serving printed in 1664, states that not much instruction is necessary for carving a ham. An illustration shows that the crackling crust needs to be folded back before slicing, as is demonstrated in both ham paintings (see cat. 10).

These paintings also show that ham is served with mustard, an herb known to the ancient Romans. Mustard was made at home, or purchased from the "mustard man," (sometimes a woman) who would sell the product door to door. This condiment can easily be prepared at home. White mustard with yellow seeds and black mustard with dark reddish-black seeds are used singly or combined and crushed with verjuice or vinegar to make a paste, which can be further flavored with honey, herbs, and various seasonings. A simple mustard recipe can be found in the cookbook.   PGR

24 Jan Davidsz. de Heem (1606–c. 1683)
Still Life with a Glass and Oysters

Dutch, c. 1640

oil on wood panel; 9⅞ x 7½ inches

signed (at upper right corner): "J. De heem"

The Metropolitan Museum of Art; purchase, 1871. (71.78)

LIGHT PLAYS upon the limpid surface of the two oysters in their opened shells and on the slice of lemon meant to add tang to this repast. It caresses the cluster of white grapes, sparkles on the curling lemon peel draping out of the *berkemeier*, and glances off the grape stems and leaves. Light shimmers on the surfaces of the rounded raspberry prunts of the glass, and through the transparent liquid. A tiny portrait of the artist is reflected in the wine. The objects have been skillfully arranged on an olive green cloth draped over a wooden table fronting a plain brown wall. Curving lines and rounded shapes abound. A monochromatic palette of yellow, brown, green and white has been judiciously applied.

For some contemporary viewers, De Heem's painting spoke of sensual pleasures to be tasted and enjoyed. For others, the wine and oysters might have signified gluttony or lust, since both were thought to serve as aphrodisiacs. None of the usual allusions to transience are present: no watch, smoking candle, smoldering embers, or knife. The absence of bread indicates a lack of religious references. This painting may simply be, as it appears, a beautiful invocation of a modest number of gustatory delights that stimulate the eye and the palate . . . and perhaps the mind.

This small signed monochromatic *ontbijtje* probably dates to about 1640 and suggests the early influence of Pieter Claesz. (see cat. 19), whose work De Heem may have seen in the early 1630s, before his first trip to Antwerp in 1636. De Heem created *ontbijtje* still lifes on laid tables as well as huge elaborate *pronk* still lifes, often featuring lobsters, musical instruments, sea shells, fruit, goblets, raised pies, parrots, moths, or butterflies. A prolific painter, he had enormous influence on many contemporary artists and attracted students from several Dutch and Flemish cities. His works were highly prized—and highly priced.　　　　DRB

ONE GETS THE IMPRESSION from the paintings in this volume that oysters were more readily available in the seventeenth century than they are in the Netherlands today, but never in the quantities found in New Netherland. There, Native Americans enjoyed the bivalves along the shores of Manhattan Island and the upper Hudson River for centuries. In fact, Pearl Street in Manhattan is named for the mother-of-pearl found in the mounds of oyster shells. Similar mounds have been found along the Hudson at Peekskill, New York. In his 1655 book, Adriaen van der Donck gloried in the oysters available in the new land, stating that large oysters, used for roasting or stewing, "fill a spoon and make a good bite." Van der Donck also claims to have seen oysters in the shell "a foot long and broad in proportion" (1968). Fresh, tightly closed oysters were packed—with sawdust between layers—in small barrels (a method that kept them edible for many weeks) and used as trade goods in the West Indies or shipped up river. In October 1665, a year after the English takeover of New Netherland, Oloff Stevensen van Cortlandt (c. 1600–1684) wrote to his son-in-law, Jeremias van Rensselaer, (1632–1674) in Albany that he had sent him "1100 oysters and 20 pounds of rice" (Jeremias van Rensselaer, 1932).

Here is *De Verstandige Kock*'s recipe for stewed oysters: "Take oysters or mussels (but the mussels have to be alive when taken from the shell), place them in a dish, place them on a chafing dish; if the mussels were cooked first add some water and vinegar or verjuice, otherwise do not. Then do add butter and mace and let it stew until [it] is done, then add some lemon juice and finely crushed rusk." See cookbook for modern recipe.　　　　PGR

25 Jan Davidsz. de Heem (1606–c. 1683)
Still Life

Dutch, 1640s
oil on panel; 14½ x 18 inches
inscribed, upper right: "Jan de Heem"
Memorial Art Gallery of the University of Rochester; Marion Stratton Gould Fund, 49.63

AN ARRAY OF TREATS is assembled on a veined marble plinth, partially draped with a blue satin cloth. A Seville orange, leaves and unopened blossom still attached, is placed next to a smoking hemp wick and some *zwavelstokjen*. Three opened oysters gleam in their pearlescent shells. An ebony-handled knife, inlaid with mother-of-pearl, projects over the edge of the table from underneath the shells. A tiny salamander crawls along its blade, hidden between the roll and shell.

A crusty white roll has been broken. Behind the roll is a silver caster, probably containing pepper to season the briny bivalves. In the center of the arrangement stands a large, raspberry-prunted *roemer* filled with white wine and garnished with a citrus, its peeled skin cascading down over the rim. A few red grapes on their stems appear between the *roemer* and caster. A laurel spray trails over the glass. A blue flower is placed near the laurel and a pansy is by the edge of the *roemer* at the level of the wine. The artist and his studio windows are reflected in the glass. Light glistens on the *roemer*, along the satin folds, and on the silver.

Did the lemon peel remind viewers to temper or moderate pleasure, like citrus cuts the flavor of sweet wine? Did the contrasting colors of the knife recall the allegory of good and evil? Perhaps the aphrodisiacal oysters and smoldering wick hinted at transient desires, while the bread and wine referred to Holy Communion. Might some think that the orange represented the Tree of Knowledge in the Garden of Eden and the salamander the tempting serpent? Or has the painter invited viewers to contemplate his skills in capturing the gritty layered texture of the shells, the crunchy crust of the rolls, and the dimpled, waxy skin of the Seville orange? De Heem may have deliberately teased the eye with curving lines and a triangular composition. However, all possibilities are implicit in the picture.   DRB

THE GLOWING ORANGE with its fragrant blossom looks as tasty as it is beautiful. The blossoms were distilled and used for orange flower water to flavor confections and sweet pastries. Oranges, imported from Curacao in the West Indies, were available in New Netherland as well. To her delight, Maria van Rensselaer (1645–1689), widow of Jeremias van Rensselaer (1632–1674) of Rensselaerswijck received six oranges from her son when he was visiting New York City in the 1670s.

Although the early varieties were sour and more pungent than eating oranges today, they added good flavor to savory dishes. *De Verstandige Kock* has a recipe for meatballs that incorporates orange zest. "It gives a very good smell and flavor," the anonymous author comments. Anne Stevenson van Cortlandt (1774–1821) of Albany, who later lived at Van Cortlandt Manor in Croton-on-Hudson, had a similar recipe in her handwritten cookbook, but she used allspice from the Caribbean, instead of the mace and nutmeg listed in *De Verstandige Kock* and hotter Cayenne pepper instead of black pepper. See cookbook for modern recipe.   PGR

26 Jan Davidsz. de Heem (1606–c. 1683) and Workshop
Still Life of Fruit, Oysters, and a Delftware Ewer

Dutch, c. 1644–1647
oil on panel; 19 x 25½ inches
Otto Naumann Ltd., New York

IN FRONT of a wall, a wooden table is covered with a dark green cloth. On top are a delicate winged wine goblet in the *façon de Venise* style, a Delftware ceramic jug, and a split red pomegranate. There are also bunches of red and green grapes on their vines.

A few shrimp and a lemon cut with a spiraling peel are on a pewter plate. Two opened oysters in the shell gleam with their succulent juices. Another pair of lemons and lemon wedges lie near the oysters. Next to the wine ewer are whole walnuts and a stray walnut meat. The grape vine tendrils create an undulating diagonal from the lower edge to the upper right of the composition. A mysterious nail protrudes from the wall at left, putting the diagonalized images into an asymmetrical balance.

Controversy abounds about the painter. Was it created by Jan Davidsz. de Heem, who used a similar jug and wine glass in a monochromatic still life (signed and dated 1648) and whose *Fruit Still Life with Wine Glass* (c. 1640–1645) also features "eaten" vine leaves, a green tablecloth, red and green grapes, a pomegranate, and a pewter plate with shrimp?

Because the handling of the paint is not as proficient as his other paintings, the picture might have been produced around 1644 by De Heem and another artist working in his Antwerp studio, perhaps Alexander Coosemans. Another possibility is Theodor van Aenvanck, who was De Heem's pupil around 1647. Whoever was responsible, the viewer could not help but marvel at the complexity of the composition, the richness of the depicted objects, the luxury of the foodstuffs, and the clever manipulation of pigment.

While Catholic viewers might associate pomegranates with the Virgin Mary, others may simply have regarded it a rare exotic fruit, seldom found in Northern European markets. Attentive observers might have looked for the reflections of the painter's studio in the glass and the shrimp's tail on the polished plate. DRB

LEMONS FEATURE prominently in many of the paintings in this book. Probably first cultivated in India, pinpointing the initial appearance of lemons in Europe is difficult. Historical records confuse the terms lemon, lime, and citron, so exact dates and places are debatable. Most historians agree that inhabitants of Spain and North Africa used lemons around A.D. 1000, while ancient Roman mosaics appear to depict lemons as early as the second or third century. Aristophanes, a Greek playwright from the fourth century B.C., noted that lemon leaves were fashioned into wreaths to crown the heads of the gods. More than one thousand years earlier, Jews were cultivating a form of citrus in Palestine, where they used the fruit as an integral part of the fall harvest celebration known as Succoth. When Jews moved to various corners of the Roman Empire, lemons began to figure prominently in Mediterranean foodways, as they do today.

Every part of the lemon is usable except the seeds and the pith. The zest, the shiny, bumpy yellow exterior containing rich lemon oil, adds intense flavor and aroma to recipes. The lemon peel adds drama to food displays as shown here. The juice accents flavors and was frequently used in sauces, while slices of lemon were added to raised pies. See cookbook for various recipes that employ lemons, including a lemon custard. PGR

27 Pieter de Hooch (1629–1684)
The Fireside (Woman and Serving Woman at a Hearth)

Dutch, c. 1670–1675

oil on canvas; 25½ x 30¼ inches

signed at the right, on the board next to the peat basket: *p. d'Hooch*

North Carolina Museum of Art, Raleigh; purchased with funds from the State of North Carolina

TWO WOMEN SHARE a domestic exchange inside a home, where a peat turf fire is blazing in the hearth. The lady of the house, seated on a low stool, holds a wooden cooking spoon, presumably to stir the contents of the cooking pot near her feet. A three-footed kettle is close by. The neatly attired servant holds a large bowl filled with creamy yellow apples. A small child sits near the fire, playing with a cat. A brown and white spaniel sniffs the servant's dark skirt.

A large wicker basket contains more peat turves. Several utensils and furnishings are depicted, including an iron skillet near the fireplace, a plate rack (barely visible at the far right), and a fringed hanging curtain at the mantel with a lobed plate, *roemer*, and other ceramic pieces atop it. A painting hangs on the chimneybreast and a framed oval portrait of a man, possibly the father of the house, is on the wall. The floor is covered with black and white marble tiles.

Leaded glass windows admit light above a cupboard bed, revealing bottles and vases on top of the cabinetry. Through a doorway at the rear of the room, an older child, wearing a *valhoedje* (a child's protective bumper hat), mounts a short flight of stairs leading to a light-filled room beyond.

Pieter de Hooch was known and admired for his perspective renderings of household interiors featuring views into adjoining rooms that draw the viewer into the picture. The doorway hints at other activities in the house. De Hooch offers a new model of life in the Dutch home, with wife and mother depicted as the center of the home, controlling the children and servants. In a republic, she is a queen seated on her simple cooking stool with a wooden spoon as her scepter. Her home is immaculately clean and well furnished with paintings and costly objects. Even the fire has been neatly laid. No doubt De Hooch's viewers were pleased to see this well-ordered *burgerlijk* (middle class) household.   DRB

THE CAREFULLY STACKED turf fire will provide steady heat, which is needed to boil some fish eaten with a sauce of Rhenish wine, water, butter, ginger, saffron, and cloves. The cooking pot at the woman's feet, having an opening of equal size to its base and two handles, is an earthenware forerunner of today's pan. The maid shows a dish of pared and quartered apples to her mistress as if to ask, "Do you think this is enough?" The apples will be added to a custard with fresh breadcrumbs and ginger, as described in the recipe below. Dutch women in New Netherland were delighted with the nut-wood used for cooking fires. "We all agree, that no turf, or other common fuel is equal to nut-wood," says Adriaen van der Donck (1968). Settlers were equally pleased with the tall oak trees they found in their new country. In letters between 1669 and 1689, Maria van Rensselaer (1645–1689) refers frequently to planks that were sawn at one of her Rensselaerswijck mills and shipped for sale to New Amsterdam (by 1664 known as New York).

De Verstandige Kock provides the following apple custard recipe. "Take Guldelingen [a sweet, gold-colored eating apple] peeled and cut into pieces, place them in a pot with water, Rhenish wine and butter thus let them simmer together, do mash them into pieces, then add to it half as much white bread, 5 egg yolks, ginger and sugar all mixed together. It is good." See cookbook for modern recipe.

PGR

28 Willem Kalf (1619–1693)
Still Life of Metal Plates with Fruit and Other Elements

Dutch, c. 1645

oil on canvas; 38½ x 33 inches

Peter Tillou Works of Art

THIS SUBDUED PICTURE was painted when Kalf was living and working in Paris. It features familiar items: a table draped with a cloth and linen napkin, pewter plates, a spiraling lemon peel, a bread fragment, olives filling a porcelain bowl, and a partially eaten filled pastry. A pomegranate, broken to reveal its juicy seeds, a dark-handled knife, a chafing dish, a cylindrical silver candle stick bearing a snuffed dark candle burned to the wick, and a tall flute filled with a glowing red wine are set on the table. A niche in the background contains a book, a box, and wine carafe. Close to the niche is a heavy drape with a tasseled tie-back. A mysterious opalescent glass globe hangs in front of the drapery, reflecting light from windows in the artist's studio.

Kalf's lemon peel, crumpled cloth, and tilted platter appear in many of his pictures. His dark background, which creates a shadowy foil for bright objects, and his control of oblique light sparkling on various surfaces, add to his genius. This picture can certainly be classified as a *vanitas*. Although the gustatory pleasures allude to worldliness, the bitter olives (associated with Christ in the Garden of Gethsemane), acidic pomegranate (associated with the Virgin Mary), and snuffed candle symbolize the brevity of life. The wine and bread fragment allude to Holy Communion.

While some viewers might have wondered what goodies were simmering in the chafing dish, others might have interpreted the brazier's coals as harbingers of the fires of hell, especially for the gluttonous. The glass ball, a reminder of *Homo Bulla* (man's life fragile as a soap bubble), also serves as a somber warning.
DRB

DUTCH PHYSICIAN Stephanus Blankaart did not see much harm in eating olives, especially if accompanied by a glass of wine. However, he was less happy with the use of pomegranates, because they were seldom sweet and ripe when they arrive in the Low Lands. Blankaart also cautioned against the use of pomegranate syrup made with sugar as quite unhealthy (1633).

The chafing dish depicted in the background on the table was used in the seventeenth century for preparing delicate dishes, as the recipe for gently stewed oysters found in De Verstandige Kock shows (see cat. 24). It was a cooking aid used by the ancient Greeks and Romans, as described in the writings of Seneca and Cicero, which is still used for preparing and warming food at the table. Other recipes in De Verstandige Kock suggest cooking food "tussen twee schotels" (between two dishes), a method that implies the use of a chafing dish, a term apparently used for both the brazier holding the hot coals and the dish containing the food.
PGR

29   Anonymous; after Willem Kalf

Still Life with Chinese Sugar Bowl, Nautilus Cup, Glasses, and Fruit

Dutch, c. 1675–1700

oil on canvas; 32 x 27 inches

The New-York Historical Society; Luman Reed Collection, New York Gallery of Fine Arts, 1858.15

LUXURY OBJECTS rest on a marble plinth, partially draped with a Persian carpet. Hazelnut shells at left sharply contrast with a Seville orange at right; the peel of a lemon cascades from an ornate silver tray.

The Wan-li Chinese porcelain bowl contains an elaborate ladle-like silver spoon. The bowl is decorated in relief with Chinese figures representing the eight "Immortals," or Taoist philosophers. The lid, with a Fu-lion (dog) finial, is propped against its side. The Fu-lion was a Chinese symbol of energy, valor, and prosperity, attributes that held significance for prosperous Dutch merchants.

Behind the bowl, is a *façon de Venise* goblet, decorated with swirled canes on the stem and lid, half filled with rosé wine. Behind the orange is a *roemer* of white wine. The nautilus cup features Neptune, god of the sea, with his trident. The shell is set in a merman mount and the strap work utilizes sea monsters. The gold-lipped rim of the shell suggests a ship's prow and the clamps a figurehead.

Dutch traders brought nautilus shells from the Indian Ocean. As early as the thirteenth century, they were set into mounts of precious metals as gifts for European royalty or high-ranking ecclesiastics. In the sixteenth and seventeenth centuries, nautilus cups were made by silversmiths in the Netherlands or imported from Antwerp and Nürnberg.

The bright surfaces and cold, hard textures of the serving pieces contrast with the warm, soft folds of the rug. While those features might have provided sufficient interest, other admirers of Kalf's work may have coveted the valuable items, prompting the artist to appeal to the vanity of clients unable to afford the luxury items depicted in this *pronk* still life.

This picture, copied by an unknown hand, replicates, detail for detail, Kalf's *Still Life with Chinese Bowl and Nautilus Cup*, 1662 (Museo Thyssen-Bornemisza, Madrid).   DRB

THE SUGAR BOWL (so large that some think it is a punch bowl), hints at the importance of sugar, ever more readily available by the seventeenth century. Initially considered medicinal, it helped make medicinal substances and foods more palatable. During the Golden Age, it became accessible to the wealthy middle class and moved from the apothecary's shelves into the kitchen.

Sugar was used for preserving fruits, herbs, and leaves, as "De Verstandige Confituur-maker" (The sensible confectioner) shows. This appendix to *De Verstandige Kock* contains twenty-six recipes for preserves; our cookbook includes several modern versions. Cinnamon bark, seeds, and nuts (see cats. 2 and 33) were among the foods preserved by coating with sugar. After being covered with hot sugar syrup, they were placed on a round, rimmed tray and shaken. As they cooled, the coating hardened. The comfits would keep for a long time. They were served with wine as a treat and a digestif at a meal's end.

Here is a recipe for candied quince squares from "De Verstandige Confituur-maker," the second appendix of *De Verstandige Kock*: "Take whole quinces, rub them clean, cook them in water, let them boil unpeeled until they are soft, take them out, cover them with a cloth until they are luke warm, remove the skins also the core and the hard parts and mash them [the quinces] very fine, take as much sugar as [you have] quince pulp, mix together and place on the fire, let it boil; when it has been boiled sprinkle a clean board with sugar and place it on there, form little cakes. Let them cool, place them on a *stoof* with fire [a foot warmer containing a pipkin with hot coals] until they are dry; you can save them in clean paper as long as you please." See cookbook for modern recipe.   PGR

30 Roelof Koets (c. 1592–1655)
A Fruit-filled Pastry, Fruits, Glasses, and Plates

Dutch, early 1640s

oil on canvas; 29⅛ x 42⅛ inches

Private collection

PRESSMARKS are plainly visible on the linen cloth covering this laid table. A silver plate holding a peach sits on top of the crumpled napkin and an engraved silver beaker, lying on its side, rests nearby. Next to the beaker is an overturned pewter jug with an open lid. Bunches of freshly cut white grapes, with leaves and curling tendrils still intact, stretch across the table. A *bekerschroef* (gilt goblet holder), decorated with the rotund figure of Bacchus, supports a *berkemeier* filled with white wine. Nearby is a pewter plate of olives, a sliced roll, a few nuts, and a knife in a leather sheath.

A Wan-li Chinese porcelain bowl contains peaches, gooseberries, and red, white, and black currants. Near the bowl, a few red and white raspberries are interspersed among leaves. A pewter dish holds a filled pie, its crust broken by a silver spoon to reveal a mixed fruit filling with a slice of lemon. An octagonal Venetian style *vleugelglas* (winged glass), half filled with rosé wine, stands behind the pie.

Warm light, introduced from the left of this subtly monochromatic still life, highlights the pewter, silver, and gilt serving pieces. Reflections abound: the beaker's base on the silver plate, the peach on the chalice and plate rim, grape leaves on the curves of the pewter jug; even Koets's studio windows are ingeniously reflected onto the plate from a reflection in the *berkemeier*.

Viewers must have been delighted with the warm tones of this picture, especially the blush on the peaches, the rosé wine, and the red berries. Some might have imagined the friendships such a luxurious dessert table bespoke.

Koets often collaborated with Pieter Claesz. (see cat. 31), and elements of his imagery are present here: the knife case, Bacchus, the overturned jug, the beaker or chalice, the roll, and reflections of the artist's studio are all found in pictures by Claesz. Filled pies occur in works by Claesz. and Willem Claesz. Heda, suggesting the influence of both Haarlem masters on Koets. DRB

THE PIE, filled with assorted berries topped with lemon slices, was covered with a top crust sprinkled with sugar, (see the strawberry *taert* [sweet raised pie] recipe in the cookbook). Berries were used in *koeldranken* (cooling drinks). The fruits flavored sauces, wine, or beer, and, when prepared with sugar as syrups, were consumed for their medicinal properties. In New Netherland raspberries were made into a raspberry liqueur (see cookbook).

Whether sweet or savory, pies were baked in a *taertpanne* (Dutch oven; see cat. 54). Separate pans were often used for *taert* (sweet raised pie) and *pastey* (savory raised pie) so that flavors would not mingle via the cookware. The recipes for *taert* are confusing because they sometimes contained meat or vegetables, but, like minced meat pie, the overall flavor was sweet. Savory pies were filled with an assortment of foodstuffs (see cookbook) and were frequently made by the *pastey backer*, often the town's caterer. They were frequently served at banquets in medieval style, decorated with feathers. Peacocks and swans were favorites for such displays because of their beautiful plumage.

These pies were used as showpieces and for entertainment, rather than as food. If consumed, the filling was ladled out because the hard and sturdy crust, which supported the decoration, was unappetizing. No doubt that is the origin of the Dutch expression (in translation) "For the lack of bread, you eat the crust of raised pies," meaning that you do what you have to do. PGR

31 Roelof Koets (c. 1592–1655) and Pieter Claesz. (c. 1597–c. 1661)
Breakfast Still Life

Dutch, c. 1650

oil on panel; 29⅛ x 39½ inches

Otto Naumann, Ltd., New York

A TABLE has been laid with red and white tablecloths. Three full *berkemeier* wine glasses are standing on a silver *puntschotel* (pointed presentation tray). An overturned glass rests on the tray near a sliced crusty roll. The black handle of a knife projects slightly over the table's edge. A pewter plate bears an overturned, cooked North Sea crab, while next to it stands a spouted wine jug, now known as a "Jan Steen" jug. A partially peeled lemon sits on another pewter plate, its skin spiraling downward and over the table. An engraved silver chalice also lies on its side in front of a tall flute half-filled with white wine. Bunches of red grapes and vine leaves are grouped at the far right, a few grapes resting atop a crumpled white linen napkin.

For religious viewers, the chalice might have recalled a communion cup, especially when seen with grapes and bread. Other viewers might have focused on the beauty of the objects and the silversmith's talents. We can only speculate on contemporary reactions to the crab. Some viewers might have recalled Roemer Visscher's emblem of the crab with dice and playing cards, admonishing parents to avoid teaching their children to gamble, while others might have smacked their lips, anticipating the succulent taste of crabmeat, piqued with lemon juice and washed down with wine.

Probably Koets, who specialized in grapes, was responsible for painting them. It is difficult to determine who painted the other elements. *Berkemeier* glasses appear in another *pronk* picture of theirs signed only with Claesz.'s initials, and he repeated the crab motif in a 1644 still-life arrangement. The rolls, chalice, and black knife handle are likewise seen in another still life by Koets (see cat. 30). Claesz. and Koets collaborated on at least five other pictures. They were joined by Jan Jansz. den Uyl, probably around 1639, in creating a still life featuring *roemers*, a beaker, a lemon, a ham, a mustard pot, and a candlesnuffer. But regardless of artist or signature, buyers were eager to own beautiful paintings like this for ornamentation or to foster reflective meditation.   DRB

THE COOKED CRAB shown in this painting would have been enjoyed with the white wine and white bread portrayed with it. The recipe from *De Verstandige Kock* suggests stewing crabmeat with butter, herbs, and spices in its own shell. That could be done because the common European crab, with a shell of about ten inches across, is larger than its American West Coast Dungeness cousin. Here is the recipe: "Remove (after they have been cooked until done) all the dirt from the crab or lobster, add to it parsley cut fine, pepper, mace, nutmeg, and butter. Stir it together until it is done. At that moment lemon juice or verjuice is added; when it is a crab it is generally stirred or stewed in its own shell." See cookbook for modern recipe.   PGR

32 Carstian Luyckx (1623–after 1670)

A Sumptuous Still Life with a Gilt Cup and Glass Holder, Silver Beaker, Nautilus Shell, Fruit, and Oysters

Flemish, c. 1660

oil on copper; 20 x 14½ inches

signed on the plinth: "Carstian Lui [*] ckx"

Private collection; courtesy of Otto Naumann Ltd., New York

A WOODEN TABLETOP, covered with a green cloth, has been laid with luxurious tableware and costly delicacies. Banquet foods include oysters, grapes, mulberries, plums, apricots, shrimp, and hazelnuts. The Chinese porcelain bowl, pewter platter, and engraved silver chalice take second place to an overturned silver gilt *akeleipokal* (German for "grape cup"), its lid decorated with a *Miles Christianus* (Knight of Christ), said to be a protector and defender of the faith. A towering *bekerschroef* (gilt goblet holder) holding a raspberry-prunted *berkemeier* filled with white wine, and a lustrous, polished nautilus shell complete the sumptuous array. The *bekerschroef*'s ornate base features a mythological scene of Venus and Mars.

All these elements bespeak elegance and wealth, especially the precious metals, which shine against the background. An *akeleipokal* and a *bekerschroef* would have been prized for their workmanship, since only highly skilled goldsmiths produced them. A *bekerschroef* was handed around at feasts to confirm the importance of friendship and the good taste of the host.

Silver beakers or chalices were associated with Communion services, but wealthy people also used them as goblets for celebratory occasions, as evidenced by the number depicted in still lifes, notably those by Roelof Koets and Pieter Claesz. (see cats. 30 and 31).

The nautilus shell bespeaks luxury, too. These chambered denizens of the Indian Ocean were prized by shell collectors. Sometimes they were set into ornate fittings and used as goblets. (see cat. 29) Often, however, the unadorned shell was admired in a wealthy owner's *kunstkamer* (art collection room) with other rarities.

Luyckx's viewers *might* have detected a caution in this lavish presentation, but more likely they thoroughly enjoyed it, marveling at the blush coloration on the shrimp, nautilus, and fruits and the greens on the hazelnut husks, apricot leaves, grapes, and tablecloth. For all its richness, the artist used a limited palette and judicious highlights. DRB

A CERTAIN AMOUNT of competition existed among Dutch country house owners as to who could produce the first, the best, or the largest exotic fruit or vegetable. The very wealthy had orangeries, where they raised orange and lemon trees in tubs. They also grew fragile peaches and apricots, and even such tropical fruits as pineapples, which had been brought to the Netherlands by the mid-seventeenth century. Nicolaes de Vijgh boasted about his *ananas van Brasiliaenschen stam* (pineapple of Brazilian origin), on his estate, Ubberge, near Nijmegen. Others, including Pieter de la Court, grew several varieties, notably one imported from Suriname in South America.

In New Netherland settlers also planted the kinds of fruits portrayed here, but theirs had to be imported from the homeland. In July 1658, Jeremias van Rensselaer (1632–1674) sent a large order to the Netherlands requesting peach stones, white plums, well-bearing sour cherries, apricot pits, large nuts, and hazelnuts. Peaches adapted well to the climate. In 1749, visiting Swedish botanist Peter Kalm marveled that roaming pigs gorged themselves on the fruit (1987). Those roaming pigs were the ones that inadvertently had planted the trees everywhere!

With an increasing supply of sugar from the Caribbean, the fruits were preserved for winter. "De Verstandige Confituur-maker" (The sensible confectioner) supplies such a recipe for peaches: "Take apricots, peaches, or plums of each a pound . . . and cook it together ["with sugar" is missing here] until the thickness of a medium syrup, let it cool and save in pots, is good." See cookbook for modern recipe.

PGR

33 Matthijs Naiveu (1647–1726)
The Newborn Baby

Dutch, 1675

oil on canvas; 25¼ x 31½ inches

signed and dated (lower left): "M: Naiveú F./1675"

Metropolitan Museum of Art; purchase, 1871. (71.160)

A WOMAN, dressed in a fur-trimmed robe over her white shift, sits upright in a large bed hung with luxurious green curtains. She has recently given birth to the baby, wrapped in swaddling clothes tied with pink ribbons, that is held by a female visitor. An elderly servant, bearing a bowl of porridge, approaches the mother, offering her nourishment, just as a little girl offers the infant a sweetmeat.

Next to the bed stands a table covered with green and wine-colored cloths and a Persian rug on which have been placed a glazed white stoneware ewer, a small round silver box, a glass-topped *roemer* filled with wine, and a pewter plate bearing a *zottinnekoeck* (a pastry filled with sugary comfits). An ornamental plaster Cupid is suspended over the bed, indicating that this child was conceived in love. A woven wicker cradle has a sumptuous dark green cloth as a cover. All these elements bespeak a house of wealth and privilege. The visitor, whose curly hair is stylishly arranged, is very fashionably dressed.

At right, the draperies have been pulled back to reveal another room where men have gathered. The father, smoking a pipe, is joined by three guests who are congratulating him with drinks.

There is a narrative quality to this painting. One can almost imagine the conversation between the new mother and her guest, hoping for the child's good health and long life, while the old woman quietly warns the mother to rest and regain her strength so she can nurse the baby. This domestic drama might have appealed to many of Naiveu's female viewers, who could identify with the experience even if their own birthing rooms were not as elegantly furnished. Male viewers, too, might have reflected on the importance of siring and raising children. The Dutch thought that children conceived in loving marriages were proof of fecundity, and also gifts from God. Naiveu began to make nursery scenes a specialty in the 1670s.   DRB

THE NETHERLANDS of the seventeenth century had several unique customs surrounding childbirth. One was to prepare a *kraamkamer* (special birthing room) for the delivery and for subsequent visits from relatives and friends. The room was outfitted with a *luiermandkast* (layette cupboard), a cradle, a *vuurmand* (dome-shaped device to dry diapers), and a *bakermat* (long, low basket, long enough to accomodate a person with outstretched legs) in which the mother (or the wet nurse) would nurse the baby by the fire. A screen was placed in front of the door and the bed hung with costly draperies to keep the new mother warm and snug. A midwife and dry nurse, and sometimes a physician, assisted with the delivery. In an era of high death rates it is no wonder that mothers and babies were pampered and celebrated.

In Naiveu's work, the mother is being served a porridge, probably flavored with anise, which was thought to encourage the flow of her milk. Also portrayed is a celebratory drink called *kandeel*, which was served to visitors, with *suikertjes* (sugar candies)—in this case candied cinnamon sticks—presented in a dish-shaped pastry, akin to rusks, called *zottinnekoecken* (see cat. 40). In later years, these pastries were replaced by rusks. Rusks with comfits are still a traditional treat at the time of a birth.

Adriaen van der Donck remarked that Native American women in New Netherland recovered almost immediately after the delivery and wondered if Dutch women were too pampered (1968). Several of the Dutch American handwritten cookbooks include recipes for *condale*, the Anglicized phonetic spelling of *kandeel*. De Verstandige Kock's recipe follows: "Take a pint of water and a pint of Rhenish wine, beat 6 eggs without the membranous thread very well, stir them together, place it on the fire until it comes to a boil. Do add to it sugar, mace, nutmeg, cinnamon and cloves." See cookbook for modern recipe.   PGR

34 Caspar Netscher (c. 1635–1684)
The Slaughtered Pig

Dutch, 1662

oil on panel; 14½ x 12 inches

Otto Naumann Ltd., New York

THE CLEANED CARCASS of a slaughtered pig, its hind and forelegs spread apart, hangs from a wooden ladder. A cord has been run through a hind leg, tying the animal to the rungs. A tall batter jug, with a wooden spoon protruding from it, sits on the tiled floor.

The animal has already been bled and disemboweled with only its two kidneys left in place. The decapitated pig's head rests in a shallow wooden tub on a stool by the carcass. A small boy, crouching behind the pig's snout, uses a straw to inflate the pig's bladder. This filled bladder, slippery with intestinal fluids, could be tossed like a balloon or squeezed to make rude noises by compressing the air through the organ's narrow neck. Children, usually boys, blowing or tossing inflated bladders were thought to be pictorial subjects akin to children blowing soap bubbles—references to *Homo Bulla* (the fragility of human life) and the transitory nature of human pleasures. Did Netscher intend for his viewers to be reminded of life's brevity? Or was he summoning up a familiar image of November, the month when nut-fattened hogs were slaughtered and preserved as a meat source for the winter? Were squeamish viewers appalled by the headless carcass? Or might not the viewer have admired the artist's and the butcher's skills in the details of the pig's white skin, singed and scraped clean? Perhaps some might even have imagined the irony of the pig's snout "smiling" at the boy's antics? Connoisseurs might have been struck by Netscher's skillful use of a limited palette of white, red, pink, black, and brown tones. Slaughtered animals hanging on ladders, often pigs but occasionally oxen, were frequent images in Dutch genre painting.   DRB

THE PIG IS slaughtered and hung for twenty-four hours to drain its blood. "One shall kill the pig in the first quarter or during the waxing of the moon," advises "De Hollantse Slacht-tijdt" (The Dutch butchering time), the first appendix to *De Verstandige Kock*. It also suggests that the pig not be fed or given water twenty-four hours beforehand, so the meat will be "better and tastier to eat." Pork was considered healthful and often prescribed for the sick.

After it was drained, the pig was cut into pieces and placed in brine, where hams and shoulders remained for nine to ten days before being hung in the chimney to be smoked. The back, sides, and feet were used in stews or soups (see cookbook). The head was cut in half and salted as well, but head meat was also boiled, seasoned, and placed in beer-vinegar to make pickled pork. The tenderest meat was on the jawbone, which was smoked to make *kinnebacks-hammetje* (little jawbone ham). The seventeenth-century book on carving recommends that when carving a swine's head at the table, one should insert a two-pronged fork in the nostrils to steady it and cut thin slices along the neck and then the jawbone hams. If that does not yield enough meat, the ears may be sliced, but generally they are left intact so the head looks better on the platter.

Pigs featured prominently in New Netherland lore. They roamed free, causing damage to public and private property alike. Period records of court cases and ordinances show that pigs even uprooted the walls of the fort in New Amsterdam.

                    PGR

35 Jan Olis (1610–1676)

Interior with Soldiers Smoking and Playing Cards in a Tavern

Dutch, 1641

oil on panel; 15⅞ x 21⅜ inches

dated at bottom on box: "1641"

Mr. and Mrs. Harry Judson Moore, Judson Galleries Inc.

SIX LONGHAIRED SOLDIERS relax in a tavern. Three are seated, two playing cards, using an overturned drum as their table. A large stoneware drink bottle and pipe are on the floor, close to the foot of an officer. Hat in his hand, one officer smokes a Gouda clay pipe. Two kibitzers stand near the card players, no doubt offering strategic advice, congratulating good plays, and mocking ineptitude. The sixth soldier, his back to the card game, is seated near the fireplace, smoking.

One of the standing officers, his back to the viewer, wears a *kolder* (a buffalo hide sleeveless jerkin), a garment favored by soldiers, who often disguised its noxious smell with perfume. His accoutrements include a sword, a hat sporting a jaunty ostrich feather, and tall leather boots. The soldiers all wear flat lace collars, which became fashionable when men grew their hair long and stopped wearing high ruffs. A dandified officer wears rose-colored shoe ribbons, laces, and garters. He displays his winning ace to the viewer.

The *coortegardje* (guardroom scene) was painted by several Dutch artists. The Netherlands used mercenary troops. Because there were long periods of inactivity, soldiers had time to squander. They were usually depicted in their barracks or in taverns, gambling at *tric trac* (a form of backgammon) or cards, or merrymaking with women and wine. Seldom were they depicted in battle, although some artists created pictures of soldiers plundering households and harrying peasants. Soldiers and military officers were usually subjects for satire, whether by painters or playwrights.

In this picture Jan Olis has effectively utilized the brown and gold colors of cured tobacco. No doubt his viewers could almost smell the smoke from the tobacco, which the Dutch "sauced" to increase its flavor. Whether they saw this painting as a comment on military life or just as a typical tavern scene is open to speculation. 　　DRB

BY THE 1620s, smoking had joined drinking as a favored addictive Dutch pastime. One foreign traveler remarked: "The smell of the Republic was the smell of tobacco." Early in the seventeenth century tobacco was grown in Amersfoort and its environs and around Nijkerk, where glass-covered seed beds, as used in the cultivation of melons, ensured germination and extended the growing season. This coarser Dutch tobacco was mixed with imported Virginia tobacco to produce a cheaper blend. Processed leaves were often "sauced" with flavorings such as anise, nutmeg, vinegar, or beer, the same sort of seasonings found in sauce recipes in *De Verstandige Kock*. Today, pipe tobacco is still spiced—with vanilla, for instance.

Blended tobacco was one of Amsterdam's most important trade products; in the 1670s some six million pounds of Dutch/Chesapeake tobacco was sold in the domestic market there and shipped throughout Europe. This prompted the remark by Claude Saumaise (related by Roelof Murris) that the Dutch Republic was "a country where demon gold is seated on a throne of cheese, and crowned with tobacco" (Murris, 1925).

This painting depicts white clay pipes, which might have come from Gouda in the province of Holland. Half the work force of that city was at one time employed in the pipe industry. Pipes were sent to New Netherland for trading and the settlers' use. Tobacco was also an important trade good in the colony. New Amsterdam became a major transit harbor, especially for tobacco grown in Virginia and Maryland; the tobacco passing through New Amsterdam was carefully regulated by inspectors who attested to its quality, since this precious commodity was often used as a means of exchange. 　　PGR

36 Jan Olis (1610–1676)

Kitchen Scene with a Still-life Arrangement of Fish, Fruit, and Vegetables

Dutch, c. 1647

oil on canvas; 25½ x 29¼ inches

Peter Tillou Works of Art

A KITCHEN MAID with a work board on her lap is gutting and preparing fresh fish removed from an earthenware pot on the floor. Muscled forearms and sturdy fingers indicate that she is capable of hard work.

A silvery cod, a thornback ray, and two smaller fish are heaped on the floor. Several pike are draining in a shallow colander, which rests atop a barrel draped with a white cloth. The woman has turned toward a man holding a stoneware jug, who seems to have interrupted her work. He is modestly attired in brown clothes and a wide-brimmed hat. The drab colors applied to this figure blend with the background elements, focusing attention on the maid and foodstuffs.

The kitchen is well stocked with additional cooking utensils, including a redware saucepan with a pouring lip, a large copper cauldron, and a double-handled storage pot. A brass skimmer hangs on the back wall, and a mortar and pestle rests upon a ledge. A glazed earthenware jar sits on another shelf near the doorway.

An apple, a large green-and-orange-skinned squash (or pumpkin), two artichokes, and a cabbage await preparation. A still life of a quince, peaches, bunches of grapes, two dark-skinned gourds, a cauliflower, and a brass shopping pail filled with apples is arranged on a nearby table. Close at hand is the maid's glass beaker of beer.

Many Dutch kitchen scenes feature women interrupted by boys or men, who are seldom depicted at work in kitchens, except for Brekelenkam's image of the old man scaling fish (see cat. 16). Occasionally, men in kitchens were thought to represent the Prodigal Son (see cat. 7). The tendency to view men as interlopers in the kitchen reflected traditional beliefs about gender roles. Hendrick Bloemaert did create an image of a man cooking, however. His Poultry Cook of 1634 is probably a picture of a professional chef employed in a wealthy household (Centraal Museum, Utrecht).

Whether or not Olis's audience thought a woman's place was in the kitchen, viewers must have admired his handling of the textures, colors, and shapes of the foods, utensils, and costumes, especially the folds of the maid's skirt, tucks in her apron, and fall of her opened chemise, as well as the way he captured the wispy quality of her hair.   DRB

THE WOMAN CLEANING the fish has quite a few vegetables available to add to her meal, such as pumpkins (see cat. 9 and 44) and cauliflower, while the fruits might be used in a *taert* or as a snack. Artichokes were a seventeenth-century aphrodisiac often given to young married folks.

Although cauliflower is one of the few vegetables not reported by Adriaen van der Donck as growing in the kitchen gardens of the settlers, it must have grown in New Netherland as well. Rensselaerswijck patroon Jeremias van Rensselaer (1632–1674) ordered cauliflower seed from the Netherlands in July 1658 for his kitchen garden.

In the seventeenth century a distinction was made that still exists today between "coarse vegetables," among them cabbages and onions, and "fine vegetables," such as cauliflower and spinach. De *Verstandige Kock* suggests stewing both cauliflower and Savoy cabbage (a curly form of cabbage) as follows. "One takes cauliflower or Savoy cabbage after it has been cleaned and cooked until well done and stews it with mutton broth, whole pepper, nutmeg, salt, without forgetting the excellent butter of Holland. A hard-boiled egg yolk which has been rubbed fine is sometimes mixed in." A modern version of this recipe and one for artichokes braised in a sauce of wine, breadcrumbs, and cinnamon can be found in the cookbook.   PGR

37 Willem Ormea (c. 1614–1673) and Adam Willaerts (1577–1664)
Fish Heaped on the Beach

Dutch, 1659

oil on canvas on paper; 26¼ x 40½ inches

signed and dated lower left: "W. ORMEA f. 165"

New Orleans Museum of Art; gift of Lambertus Piso, 71.38

AGAINST A HARBOR LANDSCAPE showing a settlement on the distant shore and seven figures on the beach, Ormea has piled a most unusual array of sea creatures: a crab, a ray, several silver and black round fish, a flounder and two other flatfish, and incongruously, at far right, a sturgeon with its distinctive dorsal ridges. On the sand are two ordinary surf clam shells. The two exotic cone shells nearby, one with a pink interior and the other white, both native to Indo-Pacific waters, were probably from the artist's collection of favorite props.

Four fishing boats and two tall-masted sailing ships on the wave-tossed sea, like the staffage figures on the shore, are the work of Adam Willaerts, who collaborated with Ormea on this picture. Willaerts has one man hefting a basketful of mussels on a staff over his shoulder. A red-capped fisherman holds two large silvery fish by their gills. A market woman, wearing a red jacket, balances a large wicker pannier on her head and carries a basket over her arm. The galleon flies the Dutch flag from its mast and stern; a red, white, and blue banderole waves in the wind. Gun ports indicate that this ship is heavily armed with cannon.

The fish could have represented Christ's disciples for religious viewers. Others might have reflected on the economic significance of the Dutch fisheries, taking nationalistic pride in Holland's seagoing fishing fleet, or the need for man-o-wars to protect trading vessels. Viewers might have been fascinated by the more remarkable features of the sea creatures' anatomy, the bulbous body of the ray and the dorsal plates of the sturgeon being worthy specimens for a naturalist's study.

The collaboration of Ormea and Willaerts, both from Utrecht, was not unprecedented, although only Ormea signed this painting. It is intriguing that two artists from an inland city chose to specialize in sea creatures and marine paintings, but then fishing and sea trade were mainstays of the Dutch economy. DRB

THIS VOLUPTUOUS yet nightmarish display of fish heaped on a beach includes the frontal section of a sturgeon, subject of the first fish recipe listed in De Verstandige Kock. The anonymous author suggests roasting a piece of sturgeon studded with cloves, then basting it frequently with butter, and finally stewing it in wine, vinegar, cinnamon, and nutmeg.

The sturgeon was once so plentiful in New Netherland's Hudson River that it was referred to later as "Albany beef." Maria Sanders van Rensselaer (1749–1830), wife of Philip van Rensselaer of Cherry Hill, Albany, had a recipe for making "caviair" (sic) from fresh sturgeon roes, which she cut "flake by flake asunder" and placed in the sun to dry before they were "packed tightly and weighted down" (n.d.).

Shortnose and Atlantic sturgeons can still be found in the Hudson River. Male sturgeon (bulls) are sold for their meat, as are the females (cows) once the caviar is removed. "Hudson caviar," which sold in 1991 for $119 per seven-ounce container, is no longer available because sturgeon have long been overfished. In 1998, all Atlantic Coast states from Maine to Florida declared a forty-year moratorium on sturgeon fishing. For that reason an adapted recipe is not in the cookbook.

The baked cod recipe (see cat. 11) indicates that it also can be used for "sea flounder, tench, roach, and haddock." In fact it is a tasty preparation for any of the firm-fleshed fish in this painting, several of which are cod. See cookbook for modern recipe. PGR

38 Adriaen van Ostade (1610–1685)
Peasant at a Window

Dutch, c. 1660

oil on panel; 10⅞ x 8½ inches

Brooklyn Museum of Art; gift of the executors of Colonel Michael Friedsam, 34.483

A PEASANT MAN leans out of an open window framed in a niche, holding a tall hexagonal *pasglas* filled with beer. The man's full lips are parted in anticipation of the next sip but his heavily lidded eyes suggest that this is not the first glass of the day. A dark hat, set at a rakish angle, covers his head, revealing only a few strands of hair. A white lace collar, loosened at the neck, suggests that he tugged it open as he drank.

At upper left, grape vines, symbolic of Bacchus, trail around the window, implying that drink is a common feature of this man's daily life. His pose, as he leans on an elbow with face and upper torso projecting out of the dim interior, and the dark, warm tones suggest the influence of Titian and Rembrandt.

In this painting Adriaen van Ostade conforms to stereotypical Dutch attitudes about the propensity of the peasants for heavy drinking, but he does so in a gentle way. This man may be "bending the elbow" once too often, but he is not retching, or in a drunken stupor, or indulging in any of the salacious activities in which peasants were often depicted by such artists as Adriaen Brouwer, Cornelis Saftleven, or Pieter de Bloot.   DRB

THE *pasglas* with its lead coils might look like a sort of measuring cup, but it is actually one of the many different drinking game glasses of the seventeenth century. In this particular instance, the glass is filled with beer and passed around. Each person had to drink down to the next ring, and if he did not manage to do so precisely, was required to drink down to the following ring, and so forth.

Another drinking game glass was in the shape of a windmill, and included sails and a little clock. The drinker blew on the sails and was then required to drink the contents of the glass before the sails stopped turning. If not, he had to drink the number of glasses shown on the mill's clock. Game glasses, or trick glasses whose contents would spill out over the unsuspecting drinker, were particularly popular in alehouses and taverns.   PGR

39 Anthonie Palamedesz. (1601–1673)
Merry Company

Dutch, c. 1632
oil on wood panel; 15⅞ x 21¼ inches
Mr. and Mrs. Harry Judson Moore, Judson Galleries Inc.

IN THIS *bordeeltje* (bordello scene) a *viola da gamba* and bed hint at a harmonious outcome. A long-haired gentleman with goatee and mustache, smoking a white Gouda clay pipe, sits close to the bed, gesturing toward the musical instrument. His fashionable black suit, white silk stockings, and scalloped lace collar, together with the black ribbon rosettes on his shoes and garters, mark him as a man of means. He is at a table, a wine-colored cloak draped over his knee. His blonde female partner sits across the table. She, too, is fashionably dressed in a rose-colored satin gown with an ornate lace collar and cuffs. While smiling knowingly at her gentleman, she toasts him with a *roemer* of wine.

The linen covered table holds a still life of a spouted pewter flagon, knife, pewter plate, and a brazier for lighting pipes. Another woman, wearing a golden yellow garment trimmed with a lace collar, stands behind the table. On the floor is a wine cistern with a case bottle and compote of grapes. In the background, a woman strums a lute while her three male companions play a game. The men wear broad-brimmed hats and flat linen collars over their doublets. The standing figure has pink rosette garters with matching pink ribbons tied on his shoes, the height of fashion in the 1630s.

The music, drink, fruits, tobacco, gaming, and attractive women mark this *Merry Company* as a *bordeeltje*, less obviously so than the rendition by Hendrick Pot (see cat. 42) with whom Anthonie Palamedesz. apprenticed in Delft after studying with Michiel van Miereveldt. Plucking a lute was then seen as a visual innuendo for copulation, and not simply an amusing musical diversion. Grapes, associated with Bacchus, the god of wine and revelry, often symbolized debauchery. Although moralists were offended by *bordeeltjes*, there was an appreciative audience for them no matter what the predicants said.   DRB

THE HALF-FILLED *roemer* of wine the woman holds will no doubt be consumed shortly. However, *roemers* were also used as measuring cups in recipes. *De Verstandige Kock* contains several such references, including the following: "To Make a Sauce over a roast Hare, Rabbit, Veal-rib, Venison, or Beef. Take a piece of butter, a half 'roemer' vinegar, a 'roemer' Rhenish wine, pepper, clove-powder, and sugar, let this boil together until it thickens, then pour it over the roast." Sauces not only enhanced the taste or texture of a dish but also complemented or corrected the medicinal qualities of food, bringing the dish into balance and making it more healthful to eat, according to the dietary theories of the time.   PGR

40 Clara Peeters (1594–c. 1640)
Still Life with Crab, Shrimps, and Lobster

Flemish, c. 1635–1640

oil on panel; 28 x 42$^{15/16}$ inches

signed (upper left in gray): "CP. Fecit"

Museum of Fine Arts, Houston; gift of the Enthoven Foundation, 99.308

CLARA PEETERS has created an image filled with luxurious edibles and serving pieces used in the presentation and consumption of food. Her laid banquet table features six Wan-li Chinese porcelain dishes in various sizes and shapes, containing a mound of butter, a large boiled crab, and a mixture of shrimp with a few tiny crabs (one cleverly overturned to attract attention). The smallest bowl holds a brown sauce. Behind it, a huge vermilion lobster is draped across its platter. Precariously close to the edge of the table is a bowl of speckled plover and white chicken eggs. Resting on a figured damask cloth depicting the sacrifice of Isaac are three rusk-like *zottinnekoecken*, one broken apart to reveal its light and airy texture. A gilt-handled knife projects over the table edge, as does a pewter plate holding a crusty roll, partially covered by a napkin. Four hardtack biscuits are piled on the cloth at right. Vertical objects—a standing salt, a Venetian-style flute, a beer glass with lion head prunts, and a stoneware wine ewer with a pewter lid—punctuate the space between the plates. A tower of three toothsome cheeses, each different, is stacked in the center.

Viewers might have licked their lips in anticipation of the flavors and aromas to be savored in this tasty collation. A scholar might recall the biblical interpretation of the tablecloth's scene or Erasmus's proverb, in his 1544 *Adagiorum*: "*Caseum habens non eget obsonio*" (He who has cheese does not need dessert). Others beholders might have been seduced into covetous thoughts by the expensive tableware, linen, and shellfish.

Similar image of cheeses can be found in many of Peeters's "cheesestack" paintings. This female painter, who never joined the artists' guild, worked in the style of her Flemish counterpart, Osias Beert (see cat. 2). Her projecting knife handle and pewter plate with the roll influenced many Dutch painters, notably Willem Claesz. Heda, Pieter Claesz., Roelof Koets, and Maerten Boelema (see cats. 23,19, 31, and 10 respectively). Clara Peters also served as a role model for later seventeenth-century Dutch women artists, including Judith Leyster, Rachel Ruysch, and Maria van Oosterwijck.

DRB

BREAD, BUTTER, AND CHEESE complement an appetizing display of seafood and eggs. More baked goods are in the foreground. Before elaborate napkin folding became fashionable, dinner rolls (see cookbook) were draped with napkins. Next to the eggs is hardtack, the mainstay of seafarers. A New Amsterdam ordinance of 1647 set the weekly hardtack rations for ships of the Dutch West India Company at "3½ pounds of hard tack, to accompany 'stew according to circumstances,' 1 pound dried fish, 2½ pounds of pork or beef, and 1½ gills [6 ounces] of vinegar."

The pastries in the foreground are called *zottinnekoecken* in Brabant, *carsteling* in Gouda and environs, or *eierschotel* in Friesland. They get their bowl shape by being scalded in boiling water, then slashed on the bottom, and baked in a hot oven, which was sealed with clay, a tricky job even for professional bakers.

The yellow cheeses in the stack are made from cow's milk, either whole milk (with cream), or skimmed evening milk and whole morning milk, or skimmed milk only. The dark cheese in the stack might be sheep's cheese, colored with sheep's feces. Not much is known about the cheeses of New Netherland, other than a 1749 record by Swedish botanist Peter Kalm stating that settlers in the Albany area ate their bread topped with grated cheese (1987).

De Verstandige Kock lists only one cheese recipe. "Take little fresh cream cheeses and egg yolks with wheat flour and butter, make a dough[-like filling] from it, place it in your crust. It is good." See cookbook for modern recipe.   PGR

41 Egbert van der Poel (1621–1664)

A *Pancake Woman* (formerly known as *The Oyster Stall*)

Dutch, mid-seventeenth century

oil on panel; 10¾ x 10½ inches

signed bottom right: "E vander PoeL"

The Detroit Institute of Arts; gift of Mrs. James E. Scripps (09.18)

A LARGE LANTERN illuminates the pancake baker in this night scene that occurs outside an inn on a cobblestoned street. The plump woman vendor is seated on a stool behind her griddle; a crude tarp shelters her from the night air. She is cooking small pancakes, using a knife to flip them. A large jug near her feet holds the batter. On the opposite side of the grill, a young girl bends forward and piles hot pancakes into her apron to carry them away. A little dog sits attentively near her feet, hoping one might fall his way. A young boy in a large tricornered hat has his hands jammed into his pockets, perhaps reaching for coins to pay for these treats. The moon rises above the roofline of a house surrounded by dark trees. Another man, in baggy peasant garb, is walking away from the stall.

Early in his career, Egbert van der Poel depicted peasant interiors and courtyard scenes, but he is better known for his night scenes, many of which featured fires and the "Delft Thunderclap" of October 12, 1654, a disastrous explosion of the gunpowder storage magazine in Delft, in which his young daughter died. This genre picture, however, is a tranquil contrast to those other fiery disasters. His moonlight views are known as *maneschijntjes* (little moon shines) and the fire scenes were termed *brandjes* (little fires) in contemporary inventories. Another depiction of a pancake baker can be found in the painting by Jan Steen (see cat. 50). DRB

THE WOMAN HUDDLED by her lantern seems to be preparing small pancakes, known as *koexkens* or *poffen-broodt*, so named in *De Verstandige Kock*. They are probably the forerunners of the now popular Dutch *poffertjes*, or puffed silver dollar pancakes, a favorite snack and carnival treat.

In a conversation, Dr. Charles Gehring of the New Netherland Project told me that the Dutch word *koek* (generally referring to a flat, not highly risen baked good) and its diminutive *koekje* (or in seventeenth century Dutch *koeckjens* or *koecxkens*) form the root of the American word *cookie*. It is quite possible that early Dutch settlers pronounced *koekje* as "koekie," since "the *-ie* diminutive was a dialectal variation in the seventeenth century and is still a feature of western Dutch dialects." The word *koekje*, in various spellings, is also used for small items fried in a *koekepan*, or pancake pan, and for any small sweet morsels like candied quince squares (see cookbook), which are called in Dutch *quee-koeckjes*, or "quince cookies."

The following recipe from *De Verstandige Kock* is for *koeckxens* (literally "cookies," but in this case best translated as fritters); they taste like fried cookies. "Take a bread that is about 3 or 4 days old, grate it very fine, then soak it in sweet milk until it is thick and has absorbed the liquid, then take some rosewater and sugar and 6 or more eggs according to how much bread you have (some take also some currants and cinnamon with it) and then fry in butter. Everyone [can make them] as big as he desires." See cookbook for modern recipe. PGR

42 Hendrick Pot (c. 1585–1657)
Scene in a Bordello

Dutch, early 1630s
oil on panel; 14½ x 19 inches
New Orleans Museum of Art; bequest of Bert Piso, 81.265

THE SCENE for seduction has been set. The round table bears the remains of a meal: a *berkemeier*, flute, pewter jug, two pewter plates, and a crumpled white napkin. Oyster shells, once receptacles of aphrodisiacal meat, litter the tiled floor. At center stage sits an officer in high boots decorated with star spurs. His cloak and rapier sword are draped carelessly on a chair. A young woman is perched on his knee, and the soldier lasciviously caresses her while wrapping his hand around her waist to part the gown over her skirt. An old crone is encouraging this seduction for a fee. Behind the procuress, a bed with curtain coverings parted slightly, anticipates the next act.

Although the Dutch did not condone adulterous alliances or prostitution, they recognized their inevitability. Nonetheless, prostitution was condemned from the pulpit and often regulated by municipal authorities through fines, jail terms, flogging, or banishment. Whores existed in every class, and at every price. High-class prostitutes, often of French or English origin, worked the *musicos* (inns for playing or listening to music, and dancing). Clients lower on the social scale enjoyed abandoned peasant girls or compliant housemaids sacked after their employers had grown tired of them.

Zalet-juffers (high-priced courtesans) were immortalized by writers in *kluchtspelen* (bawdy comedies) that poked fun at their ways, as they triumphed over lustful men. Painters satirized them with bordello scenes. Often, as depicted here, the men were military officers. Perhaps a "slice of life" for soldiers away from their wives and sweethearts? Or a sarcastic jape at the morality of mercenaries, "patriots for hire" recruited into the Dutch army from England, Germany, France, and Scandinavia?

The borderline between "merry company" and "bordello" scenes was never firmly drawn. But the affectionate diminutive *je*, meaning "little," attached to the *bordeeltje* when listed in inventory accounts, indicates the relatively innocuous light in which this subject was regarded.   DRB

THE OYSTERS in this painting were eaten for their presumed arousing effects. Abundantly available in New Netherland, oysters there were used for a more prosaic purpose: they were sent to the West Indies as trade goods. Oysters were also shipped from New Amsterdam up the Hudson River to Esopus (Kingston) or Beverwijck (Albany).

Instead of being reserved for seduction, oysters were enjoyed by colonists at regular meals. With the exception of the cookbook of Maria Lott Lefferts of Brooklyn (1786–1865), which is devoted to dessert recipes, all of the handwritten cookbooks by descendants of the settlers present oyster recipes. Elizabeth Ann Breese Morse (d. 1828), the mother of artist and inventor Samuel F. B. Morse (1791–1872), lists two recipes for oyster sauces and one each for fried oysters and oyster "pye." In her handwritten cookbook, Maria Sanders van Rensselaer (1749–1830) of Cherry Hill, Albany, noted that she stewed oysters by themselves or with bass, which was partially cooked on a gridiron. She also fried them rolled "in fine Indian meal [cornmeal]" (n.d.). One of her daughters, Elizabeth (1770–1798), pickled them. So did fellow Albany native Anne Stevenson van Cortlandt (1774–1821), who fried, collopped, and stewed them, as well as using the bivalves for soup and a sauce.

A straightforward recipe for stewing oysters, from Maria Sanders van Rensselaer's handwritten cookbook, follows. "To stew oysters. Take 1 pint of oysters, set them over the fire in their own liquor with a glass of wine, a lump of butter [use 4 tablespoons], some salt, pepper and mace. Let them stew gently" (n.d.). This recipe needs no modern adaptation. Just do not overcook the oysters or they will be rubbery.   PGR

43 Hubert van Ravesteyn (1638–before 1691)

Still Life of a Flower, Glass, Stoneware Jug, and Walnuts in a Chinese Bowl on a Ledge

Dutch, c. 1670

oil on canvas; 28 x 23½ inches

signed with monogram in center of ledge: "H.R."

Peter Tillou Works of Arts

A RED AND WHITE marble ledge, partially draped in blue satin, supports a large pink rose, its petals fully opened and leaves still attached. Next to the rose, is a Wan-li Chinese porcelain bowl filled with walnuts in their shells. A cracked nut, with half its shell removed, is next to an ivory-handled knife, which protrudes from beneath the cloth and projects over the ledge. A discarded walnut shell is also on the ledge. Behind the porcelain bowl stands a white *Enghalskrug* (in German, a narrow-necked stoneware jug), its silver lid gleaming against the dark background. A tall *façon de Venise* flute, glowing with red wine, is next to the jug. Hubert van Ravesteyn signed this painting with a gold monogram at the center of the marble edge.

Viewers attuned to emblematic resonances might have interpreted the walnuts and wine as symbols of Christ or picked up the long association of the rose and blue cloth with the Virgin Mary. Connoisseurs of art, on the other hand, might have evaluated the painting simply as a pleasurable presentation of sensory delights, imagining the floral fragrance, the sweet taste of the wine, and the bitter flavor of the walnuts. Still other viewers might have regarded the work as an allegory on the senses of taste, smell, and sight. All of these interpretations are possible.

Van Ravesteyn used a similar bowl of walnuts and *Enghalskrug* in a 1670 painting that also featured a pipe, packet of tobacco, and flute of wine, but in that work, the red marble top is draped with a purplish red cloth.   DRB

WALNUTS AND OTHER varieties of nuts are often portrayed as accompaniments to a glass of wine. When picked young, before the outer shell hardens, walnuts can be candied in sugar syrup and used with other sweetmeats at the end of the meal.

The patroon Jeremias van Rensselaer (1632–1674) ordered "large nuts" to be sent from the homeland for planting on his estate at Rensselaerswijck. Nuts were also pickled in New Netherland. In her handwritten cookbook, Anne Stevenson van Cortlandt (1774–1821), an Albany native of Dutch ancestry, used walnuts picked "about the 20th of June," seasoned them with mustard seed, cloves, nutmeg, garlic, and horseradish, and steeped them in vinegar. The pot was sealed with a bladder and allowed to stand in a dry place for four months before they were eaten (n.d.). Anne Macvicar—later Grant—(1755–1838), a Scottish woman who spent her youth with the Dutch American Schuyler family in the Albany area in the 1760s remembers "nuts ready cracked" being served at the late afternoon meal with tea (Grant 1809). Other diarists reported that nuts and apples were offered as refreshments to visitors.

A recipe for candying unripe walnuts is found in "De Verstandige Confituur-maker" (The sensible confectioner), the second appendix to *De Verstandige Kock*. "Pick the nuts on St. John's Day [June 24] before the pit is hard, with a small pin prick several holes in them, soak them for 9 or 10 days and refresh [the water] often then boil in a little water and then boil in sugar or syrup, but at least four times as long as for lemons or orange, when the membrane is removed and cloves or cinnamon have been stuck in them, cook them adding some honey or sugar once in a while as they boil away, then leave in the syrup. You can keep them for a long time this way." See cookbook for modern recipe.   PGR

44 Pieter Cornelisz. van Rijck (c. 1568–c. 1635)
Market Scene

Dutch, 1622

oil on canvas; 49¾ x 58½ inches

North Carolina Museum of Art, Raleigh; purchased with funds from the State of North Carolina

A BEARDED FARMER, bearing a sturdy splint basket filled with pumpkins and squash, arrives at a market stand where a woman is arranging produce and live poultry for sale. The man, dressed in dark clothing, sports a fur hat adorned with hops and gooseberries. The rosy-cheeked vendor, wearing a dark bodice over her blouse and an apron to protect her skirt, has her sleeves rolled up, revealing strong arms. The neckline of her blouse is open, showing a plump décolletage.

The table top in front of the woman is piled with produce—chicory, fava beans, white carrots, salisfy, green beans, artichokes, and knobby Jerusalem artichokes. A wicker basket brims with grapes, apples, pears, and melons. A turkey stands between the woman and the large cabbages behind her. A rooster and hen can be glimpsed between the couple. Behind the market vendor are baskets of lettuces, Kirby cucumbers, and some currants, and a wicker cage containing live pigeons. In front of the birds, another wooden counter is crowded with onions, white turnips, parsnips, orange carrots, a large green squash, a pumpkin, and red and white cabbages.

The rich bounty of Holland's gardens is clearly evident in this display, although the artist has taken liberties in this contrived depiction, since not all the fruits and vegetables were likely to have been harvested simultaneously. No doubt he had to sketch or paint them sequentially when in season, an approach often used by Dutch still-life painters when working with either produce or flowers.

Van Rijck, a Delft follower of Pieter Aertsen (see cat. 1) and Joachim Beuckelaer, clearly delighted in the textures, shapes, and colors of the produce, and whimsically inserted an herb in the basket of cucumbers. He leaves it to his viewers to determine whether the painting depicts a simple transaction between grower and seller or hints at flirtation and sexual innuendo. DRB

A TRULY ASTONISHING ARRAY of New World foodstuffs is mixed in with Dutch market vegetables (see cookbook). In New Netherland, Adriaen van der Donck encountered "all sorts of pumpkins and cucurbites that may be found anywhere. [T]he Spanish [mammoth] pumpkin is considered the best" (1968). That may be the same variety portrayed here (see cat. 13). Van der Donck also described what the Dutch called *quaasiens* and reported that the English called them squash—probably summer squash; "planted in the middle of April, the fruit is fit for eating by the first of June" (1968).

New and exotic plants were found in the gardens of Dutch country houses. Botanist Pieter Hondius, for instance, describes in a long poem his garden's *artisocken onder de aert* (Jerusalem artichokes), another native American plant. *De Verstandige Kock* uses these as part of an elaborate stew recipe called *olipodrigo*. The vegetable, which was thought to taste like artichoke hearts, got its name from *girasole*, a plant with flowers that follow the sun.

By the seventeenth century, turkeys had long been domesticated in the Netherlands and were featured in several recipes in *De Verstandige Kock*. "To nicely cook young hens, turkey or ducks. When they are cleaned inside and washed fill them and cram them full with parsley. Boil them only with salt and water until they are done. Take an earthenware pan, pour in some verjuice and salt [add butter], and when the butter is melted take out the parsley from the turkey, cut it [the parsley] small, add it to the verjuice and butter, stir them together well, place in a dish and the turkey on it. Is absolutely delicious." See cookbook for modern recipe. PGR

45 François Rijckhals (c. 1600–1647)
Barn Interior with a Rustic Still Life

Dutch, 1630s
oil on panel; 14½ x 19⅝ inches
remnants of a monogram and of a date "163"
Private collection

INSIDE A GLOOMY BARN, a farm woman is placing a leg of mutton into a *vleeschkuyp* (wooden preserving tub). She is working close to a ramshackle well, where a copper water bucket hangs from a pulley. Storage containers, cooking utensils, and some vegetables surround the woman. Haphazardly arranged on the barn floor are a footed earthenware skillet, an overturned, impressed stoneware jug, a wooden keg tipped on its side, a white cloth, and a brass milk can filled with straw. A *karn ton* (wooden butter churn), a wicker basket filled with radishes, a brass-lined iron cauldron with loop handles, and a wide-mouthed glazed pot are closer to her. A large red cabbage sits on the wooden ledge of the well. Debris strewn across the floor includes a broken clay pipe, a worn broom, a wood and leather *sabot* (clog), and a contraption with feeding holes for poultry. In the shadows, two bent figures—old folks seated by a sleeping dog—are barely discernible.

Rijckhals might have been making an allusion to *Prudentia*, where the *vleeschkuyp*, symbolizing the virtue of prudence, was incorporated into a print made years earlier by Pieter Bruegel. He might have intended the butter churn to symbolize effort and hard work, as characterized by the motto in Roemer Visscher's 1614 emblem book entitled *Sinnepoppen*: "In de rommelingh ist vet" (In the commotion [of churning] comes the fat).

However, the chaotic arrangement suggests that this household has been neglected; the brickwork on the well is in need of repair and the milk cannot be used for its intended purpose. Perhaps Rijckhals's wealthy urban patron enjoyed the sharp contrast between his own well-ordered household and this rural slovenliness? Some contemporaries might have understood the straw in the milk can as emblematic of foolhardiness: "trying to get cream from cattle fodder and a milk can minus the cow." Others might have detected an insulting allusion to the peasant woman's sexual availability: "as easy as stuffing straw in a milk jug."

Known for his rustic barn still-life pictures, Rijckhals was also a painter of elaborate, showy *banketje* still lifes, displaying his versatility in capturing shapes, textures, colors, diverse materials, and lighting effects of depicted objects.

DRB

A BUTTER CHURN stands in the center of the painting while a typical brass milk pitcher is portrayed in the right foreground. Butter making dates back to biblical times. According to the *Old Testament*, "Surely, the churning of milk bringeth forth butter" (*Proverbs* 30:33).

The quality of butter, which depends on its freshness and the percentage of butterfat, greatly influences the outcome of most dishes. It is an ingredient frequently found in *De Verstandige Kock*. Some recipes include admonishments like "especially do not forget the butter," or "without forgetting the excellent butter [of the province] of Holland," which was considered the best. In his *Borgerlijke Tafel*, physician Stephanus Blankaart proclaimed that "Butter is God's blessing to our country" (1633), not only for its healthful qualities but also for its importance as a trade good.

Butter was even used as a method of payment in New Netherland. When a community shepherd was hired in Harlem (Manhattan) he received a cash stipend and half a pound of butter for each cow in his flock. Butter rather than oil was used in the Netherlands and New Netherland. When Swedish botanist Peter Kalm visited the Albany area in the mid-eighteenth century he described a dish unknown to him, consisting of the finely cut inner leaves of cabbage mixed with a dressing (our present-day coleslaw). He added that for this dish "butter is frequently used," mixed with vinegar and kept warm in a pot by the fire (1987). See cookbook for modern recipe.

PGR

46 Andries Andriesz. Schaeck (1640s?–before 1682)
The Latest News (also known as *Smokers in a Tavern*)

Dutch, mid-1660s

oil on canvas; 21¼ x 19½ inches

New Orleans Museum of Art; bequest of Bert Piso, 81.278

THREE MEN are gathered in a *tabagie* (a smoking saloon). One sits on an overturned basket, holding a many-sided bottle of *genever* (Holland's gin) and a white clay pipe; another broken pipe lies on the floor. His unbuttoned brown doublet, red vest, loosely tied lace collar, and slightly opened fly suggest that he is quite tipsy—whether from drink or the effects of nicotine. He is smiling and appears comfortable enough in front of the blazing fire. A second man, seated in a ladder-back chair with hat in hand, is listening intently to a young man who reads a gazette; the listener appears to be agitated by the news. Between these two, a crude stool holds yet another pipe, a paper filled with tobacco, and three *zwavelstokjen*.

The reader wears a workman's apron over his breeches. His tall crowned hat is dented at the top, perhaps subtly signaling that reading is not his greatest talent. Next to his feet is a large glazed brown earthenware canteen, missing its handle straps. On the far wall, behind the smokers, a square-sided case bottle rests on the wooden cabinet. A painting is faintly discernible on the wall.

The painting is suffused with the warm brown tones of cured—and flavorfully sauced—tobacco. Schaeck has used a very restrained palette, only highlighting the brown tones with touches of red, yellow, and blue.

Newspapers evolved in the seventeenth century from printed bulletins and merchants' letters. Amsterdam's first paper was issued in 1618. By the end of the century, the city had four. Sundry news items of foreign courts, comets, murder, and mayhem were supplemented with lost-and-found notices, reports of thefts (often of jewelry) and accidental drownings, and with advertisements of goods and impending auction sales. It is no wonder that Schaeck's smokers and drinkers were registering astonishment on their faces. DRB

NEWSPAPERS were carefully read and discussed in the Netherlands and, whenever possible, sent to relatives in New Netherland. Jeremias van Rensselaer (1632–1674) received newspapers from his brothers in the homeland and from his brother-in-law, Stephanus van Cortlandt (1643–1700), in New Amsterdam. Van Rensselaer no doubt circulated them in turn among his upriver acquaintances. News from the Netherlands must have been precious in the colony, especially during the winter months, and was shared in taverns and inns, as portrayed in Schaeck's painting. PGR

47 Floris Gerritsz. van Schooten (c. 1585–1656)
Breakfast of Mussels, Cheese, Bread, and Porridge

Dutch, c. 1615

oil on panel; 22 x 34¼ inches

Teresa Heinz and the late Senator John Heinz

ON A LAID TABLE covered with a crisp white linen cloth edged with picots, the viewer is presented with a beer-filled waffle beaker, a Wan-li Chinese porcelain bowl containing slabs of butter, a round loaf of bread, a crusty oval roll, a redware platter filled with steamed mussels in their shells, and a small majolica bowl of sauce resting atop the mussels. There is also a an earthenware plate for the discarded shells, two slices cut from a loaf of coarse grain bread, three crunchy rusks, a standing pewter salt, and a pewter platter piled with three cheeses next to a loaf of rye bread. An earthenware porringer, its contents dripping over the rim, has a spoon in it. A knife completes the array.

This monochromatic study of simple foods has given the painter an opportunity to spatially dazzle the viewer with the roll, plate, and knife handle projecting over the edge of the table, casting dark shadows on the white cloth. The folds in the linen add textural appeal, as do the slice marks on the largest crumbly cheese.

Might this picture be an evocation of pride in Haarlem's production of beer, and in the export value of Holland's cheese and butter? Or perhaps it is a reminder of the pleasures of simple, health-giving, and satisfying foods? Certainly it provided the painter with a splendid opportunity to display the subtlety and contrast that can be achieved with black, brown, ochre, white, and yellow pigments.

Floris van Schooten is best known for his market and kitchen scenes with still-life arrangements of foods. Of the more than one hundred dated works he created between 1617 and 1644, many were breakfast pieces that repeated the motif of cheeses and butter dishes. He was clearly influenced by Clara Peeters's imagery (see cat. 40).   DRB

THE PERFECTLY FORMED *beschuit* (rusks) wait to be topped with butter or cheese; many Dutch people still finish breakfast this way today. In the seventeenth century, cheese was an important food, usually eaten at breakfast and at the early afternoon meal.

The round cheese on top has clearly been whittled away at previous meals. Physician Johan van Beverwijck's *Schat der Gezondheid* (Treasury of good health), first published in 1636, recommends salt to open the stomach and cheese to close it.

Commercial bakeries for rusks and *zeebeschuit* (hardtack) were located north of Amsterdam in the Zaanland, a shipbuilding center. The Zaanland towns of Wormer and Jisp were known for their *tafel beschuit* and hard tack production since the middle of the sixteenth century. Rusks were baked in metal rings to create the uniformity shown in this painting. They were brought to market by the barrelful and sold in quantities of one hundred, fifty, or twenty-five (which was called a *vierendeel* or quarter). It was also possible to purchase half a quarter, rounded up to thirteen pieces. Might this be the origin of the baker's dozen? *Beschuit* (known in America as "Holland Rusks") are still sold thirteen to a package in the Netherlands.

Rusks were frequently used in recipes to thicken sauces. For an appealing presentation, rusk crumbs were sprinkled on the (buttered) rim of a serving dish.

In New Netherland women had to make rusks at home. Several recipes are found in the handwritten cookbooks of descendants of the Dutch settlers, including this one from the cookbook of Anne Stevenson van Cortlandt (1774–1821): "Rusk, 3 pounds flour, 1 pound sugar, ¾ pound butter, 1 quart milk, 5 eggs, tea cup yeast" (n.d.). See cookbook for modern recipe.   PGR

48 Michiel Simons (1630-1673)
Still Life of Fruit with Lobster and Dead Game

Dutch, c. 1650s

oil on canvas; 39¼ x 56¼ inches

New Orleans Museum of Art; bequest of Bert Piso, 81.280

A FRINGED DRAPERY has been pulled back, unveiling a laid table, partially covered with a light cloth, fronting a red marble column and neutral wall. At left is an unusually small cooked lobster, one claw resting on a pewter plate holding a cut lemon, its long peel spilling over the table. The plate rim juts over the table edge, with the colors of the fruit and crustacean reflected on its surface. An over-sized, prunted *roemer* of white wine and a large Wan-li porcelain fruit bowl filled with bunches of grapes, luscious peaches, and a quince are next to the plate. Grape vines and leaves are tucked among the fruit.

Several dead game birds are presented, including a string of small birds, a partridge, and a mallard, its ringed neck dangling over the table's edge. A hare is suspended by a cord with a metal hook. Its unseeing eyes stare out reproachfully at the viewer.

Might Simons's viewers have been put off by the diminutive size of his lobster, wondering if he used a crayfish as a model? Or might they have been intrigued by the arrangement of the vine leaves angling toward the left and the fruit bowl, dangerously balanced, tilting toward the vines? Would some have seen this picture as a reflection of God's bounty to mankind, and of human dominion over the animal kingdom?

Simons combines two still-life traditions in this painting: the *pronk banketje*, featuring luxury fruits and seafood, and a game piece. Several Dutch and Flemish painters specialized in game pieces, usually depicting a hare but in some cases painting stags, swans, or wild boars. Partridges, waterfowl, and small songbirds were often included (see cats. 53, 54, 55, and 60).

Certainly Simons borrowed the spiraling rind from other artists, notably Jan Davidsz. de Heem and Pieter Claesz. (see cats. 25 and 31), just as he repeated the conventional window reflection on the roemer and the plate projecting over the table's edge. The use of drawn-back drapery was a *trompe l'oeil* technique likewise employed by many Dutch artists. Deceiving the eye of the beholder delighted not only Dutch collectors, but also an international audience.   DRB

TO CATCH SMALL SONGBIRDS like the ones portrayed in this painting, hunters actually spread glue on tree branches, sticks, or even strings, trapping the hapless birds that would land on them. Songbirds, including finches, larks, and thrush, were sold at seventeenth-century Dutch poultry markets along with pigeons, snipe, quail, peacocks, heron, and swans. These birds were roasted, or used in savory raised pie.

In New Netherland birds were extremely abundant and of great variety. An ordinance of 1652 forbade discharging firearms at partridges within the limits of New Amsterdam; it suggests that settlers would just step out their doors and shoot their supper!

De Verstandige Kock lists a recipe for finch *pastey* (a savory raised pie). "Take finches, wash them very well and boil them a little then place them in the pastey, dress them with cinnamon, sugar, currants, pine nuts, sucade [citron] and butter bake this all together for half an hour: the sauce should be Rhenish wine and sugar. A modern version of this recipe, using boned quail instead of finches, can be found in the cookbook.   PGR

49 Joris van Son (1623–1667)
Vanitas Still Life

Flemish, 1652

oil on canvas; 30 x 40⅛ inches

signed and dated (in upper left cartouche): "J. Van. Son. f 1652"

Private collection

A TABLE has been laid with a rumpled scarlet cloth that appears soft to the touch. An array of fruits, manmade objects, and a human skull has been arranged upon it. Piled atop a blue jewelry casket is a stringed cittern and two music books, one opened to favorite pieces. Seville oranges, a peeled lemon, a melon cut with petal-like slices, purple plums, green and red grapes, a quince, and a pear surround two opened oysters.

A tall flute glass, wrapped with a sprig of ivy, stands near the music next to a *bokaal* (gilt cup) topped with a finial of *Miles Christianus*, which dominates the center of the picture. Its reflective gold surfaces contrast sharply with the dark background. The human skull, crowned with laurel leaves, rests on two leather-bound volumes in front of a pistol and a smoldering hemp wick, used to light the white clay pipe. Three butterflies, symbols of immortality, inspect various objects.

No one can mistake the artist's intention in portraying the vanity of human pleasures and the irony present in such luxuries. Just as notes of music quickly fade and smoke dissipates, beautiful butterflies are short-lived, fruits rot, wine is drunk, and books are forgotten. This is a reminder that human life ends in the grave, where everyone, rich or poor, becomes a skeleton, ending the desire for lavish jewels and rich foods. The *Miles Christianus* urges religious viewers to be devout Christians and defenders of their faith.

"*Vanitas, vanitas, omnia est vanitas*" (Vanity, vanity, all is vanity) was Joris van Son's inscription on another painting pairing a skull, a pistol, the same *bokaal*, and music books, along with rare sea shells and delicate fruits.   DRB

THE MELON is artfully cut. The pieces removed might have been used for tasting, as was the custom at markets. This practice led Jacob Cats (1577–1660), the Dutch poet, to admonish his contemporaries: "*Gelijck men handelt den meloen, soo moet men oock met vrienden doen*" (The way you choose a melon, you should choose your friends) (1632; 1880). By the second half of the seventeenth century, melon beds had come into fashion. At first small and portable, they gradually became larger stationary cold frames, where melons or cucumbers were grown.

By the end of the century these frames became hot-houses, which remain a part of the landscape today in the Dutch coastal areas. Exotic plants were brought from wherever Dutch ships docked (see cat. 44). Specimens were planted in the Royal Gardens and other botanical gardens, and were acquired by private collectors as well. A definitive source of information on country house gardens is *Den Nederlantsen Hovenier* (The Dutch gardener) by Jan van der Groen, who served as gardener to William III, the Prince of Orange. This book, together with several other sections on gardening and medicine and *De Verstandige Kock* with its two appendixes, forms *Het Vermakelijck Landtleven* (The pleasurable country life), a book that might have been used by descendants of early settlers in New Netherland.

Melons are best enjoyed plain. However, a delicious recipe from *De Verstandige Kock* for a plum *taert* calls for the purple plums shown in the foreground of the painting. "Take plums, cook them until done, rub through a sieve, dress them with egg yolks, sugar and cinnamon, cloves and melted butter, place them in your crust, bake it without upper crust then sprinkle with cinnamon." See cookbook for a modern recipe.   PGR

50 Jan Steen (1626–1679)

Pancake Woman

Dutch, c. 1661–1669

oil on canvas; 26¼ x 20⁷/₁₆ inches

Memorial Art Gallery of the University of Rochester; Buswell-Hochstetter bequest, 55.71

A COLORFULLY ATTIRED woman dressed in a broad-brimmed straw hat, red jacket, white blouse, and blue-gray apron over her taupe skirt sits under a large tree. She is baking pancakes on a skillet set on a trivet above a crackling wood fire. On a nearby tabletop is a basket of nuts, half an apple, a dish of butter, and pears and apples in a small basket, with a crumpled napkin. Under the makeshift table is an earthenware batter jug with a spoon. The baker uses a knife to turn three small pancakes simmering in the sizzling pan.

The pancake maker is extending her hand to receive a coin from the blonde-haired child standing beside her. An old woman leans over the little girl, prompting her in the exchange. A wooden shopping basket slipped over her arm suggests that a marketplace is close by. An old man, possibly the grandfather, stands behind them, his dark hat contrasting with the sky and clouds. At far right, a man in a tall cap exits the scene through a doorway in the fence. All four faces occur in other paintings by Steen. It is, therefore, assumed that the child is his own daughter, Eva. Steen's friends and family would have found this an amusing touch. All his viewers probably smiled at this depiction of a familiar scene of daily life.

The pancake baker was an image that delighted Dutch collectors and homeowners alike and remained a popular theme among seventeenth-century Dutch artists; some represented pancake bakers in homes or taverns, as an allegory on the sense of taste; others painted them in outdoor market settings like this (see cat. 41). Rembrandt's etching of a pancake woman influenced Steen and many other artists. Pancake bakers are usually depicted as women, although the Flemish artist Adriaen Brouwer (who worked in Haarlem) painted a man baking pancakes in the mid-1620s. About 1665, Steen also painted *Child Pancake Baker*, where an older sister fries up pancakes for her young siblings. DRB

IN THE SEVENTEENTH CENTURY, pancakes could be purchased on the street from vendors with portable equipment as this painting and another by Egbert van der Poel (see cat. 41) illustrate. The pancakes were eaten out of hand, the way we now munch on a hot dog. Behind the brazier a batter pot is within reach, and a dish with a lump of butter stands on the table. Used to grease the pan, butter might also be slathered on the pancake before it is given to the customer.

Pancakes were sold by vendors as snacks, but at home they were served as a meal (but not for breakfast). Recipes for pancakes appear in medieval manuscripts. Since one needed only a few implements and inexpensive ingredients —flour, liquid in the form of milk or water, eggs, and butter—to prepare them, their popularity with the lower classes was ensured, although they were equally favored by the affluent middle class.

The pancake woman clearly has three pancakes in her pan. Therefore, a modern recipe for "Three in the Pan" pancakes is included in the cookbook. This differs from other pancake recipes in that yeast, rather than eggs, is used for leavening. The pancakes are small and light. Currants or small pieces of apple may be added to the batter. PGR

51 Jan Steen (1626–1679)
Twelfth Night

Dutch, 1662

oil on canvas; 51¾ x 64⅜ inches

signed and dated on stool in center: "JSteen 1662" ("JS" in ligature)

Museum of Fine Arts, Boston; 1951 Picture Fund 54.102

THREE GENERATIONS of a family celebrate Twelfth Night, or the Feast of the Epiphany, when the Three Kings from the East presented gifts of gold, frankincense, and myrrh to the infant Christ. The youngest child, wearing a paper crown, has been selected as "king" for the evening. When the celebrants shout "The King drinks!" he will raise the huge *roemer* of wine to his lips. An older boy smiles at the "king" while a second offers him a celebratory waffle. An old woman holds another waffle in a pewter plate on her lap. Egg shells and a batter jug near her chair identify her as the waffle baker. A fire burns in the hearth, where an old man fills his pipe with tobacco.

A laughing couple facing the viewer sits at the table, while a fiddler strikes up a tune. A jester, in a fool's cap, brandishes a stick (obscenely hung with egg shells and a dangling sausage) at another twosome. The man, in a Quaker-style hat, covers his eyes while his wife seems to be smiling in pained amusement. Another man, wearing a party hat and holding a tankard, sits on a bench (bearing the artist's signature), his back to the viewer. A *pasglas* of beer and a *tazza* bearing roasted chicken are on the table.

Light illuminates the faces of the celebrants with a cheery glow and is reflected on the lobed plate and gilt picture frame.

Ignoring table revelries, two children play a traditional game. The boy sits on the floor, watching the little girl who has lifted her skirt (naughtily exposing her knees and thighs). At the outer door, a woman greets three singers, carrying a star lantern.

Twelfth Night was a favorite theme of Jan Steen's, who painted at least eight different versions. The subject, popular with Catholics, traces its imagery to paintings by the Flemish artist Jacob Jordaens whose "king" was always the oldest man present. Here Steen has cleverly cast a young boy in the role, alluding to the Christ child. Steen, a Catholic, humorously immortalized many Catholic holidays and festive celebrations in his pictures of Twelfth Night, Carnival, Pentecost, the Feast of Saint Nicholas, and Easter. He frequently included the spaniel in those celebrations and scenes of daily life. 			DRB

THE FEAST OF SAINT NICHOLAS on December sixth and Epiphany on January sixth grew out of religious observances and turned into popular family celebrations. In 1574, during the Protestant Reformation, the Synod of Dordrecht decreed that only Christmas, Easter, Ascension Day, and Pentecost were religious holidays. But it was difficult to keep people from celebrating the other holidays in their homes.

The "king" and his "court" depicted here were assigned their roles in three different ways. The one used in this painting was a "king's letter." Sold cheaply by street vendors before the event, these "letters" were large pieces of paper divided into small squares with pictures and descriptions of each job. The squares were cut apart and put in a hat for drawing by the participants. The bottom of the paper formed a crown for the king. Another method was by serving a "King's bread" with a bean baked into it. The person who received the slice with the bean was pronounced king and would choose the rest of his court. Yet a third way used playing cards as a means of deciding who became the king for the night.

The children in the foreground play a special game of jumping over three lighted candles symbolizing the three magi. In the background, the door has been opened for the carolers, who show off their lighted star and will receive food or coins at the end of their rendition.

Waffles and pancakes were the traditional fare. Abundant food and drink were an integral part of the celebration. *De Verstandige Kock* has an excellent recipe for waffles, which were made in a long-handled waffle iron held over the coals in the open hearth (a trivet was generally used to steady the iron). "To fry waffles: For each pound of wheat flour take a pint of sweet milk, a little tin bowl of melted butter with 3 or 4 eggs, a spoonful of yeast well stirred together." See cookbook for modern recipe. 			PGR

52 Jan Steen (1626–1679)
Prayer Before the Meal

Dutch, c. 1667–1671

oil on canvas; 24¾ x 30¾ inches

signed lower left on brick: "JStin" (first two letters in ligature)

Philadelphia Museum of Art; John G. Johnson Collection

ON A SUMMER EVENING a peasant family sits under a grape arbor, preparing to eat a simple meal of porridge and bread. The mother, holding a suckling baby, has her hands folded in prayer over the infant's, teaching the little one to say grace before eating. Her son, hat removed respectfully, stands and glances heavenward as he prays. His father crouches on a low stool, his head bent in prayer and eyes closed, so he cannot see the sly dog licking the cooking pot on the ground.

Just as the woman has a key suspended from her waist, the "key" to this picture is the fulfillment of Christian family obligations. Indeed, Steen's contemporaries would have contended that even an infant should be grateful to God for his mother's breast milk. The pedagogic role of parents as the first instructors of their children, a belief cherished by the seventeenth-century Dutch, is a theme often used by Steen, who knew life's moral and religious lessons began at home. The pot-licking dog, however, also admonished families to pay close attention to everyday household matters. Dogs, like children, must be trained to behave properly.

This picture is one of several versions Steen devoted to the subject of saying grace, including his 1660 Prayer Before the Meal, in which he also used a barrel as a table. His image owes much to Adriaen van Ostade's etching of 1653. Steen invites not only meditation on the theme of the good life simply led, but also admiration for the painter's command of his craft and his wit. He cleverly signed this picture on a loose brick or stone, a whimsical play on his surname, which means "stone" in Dutch.   DRB

THE EVENING MEAL, which begins with prayerful thanks, consists of no more than a communal porridge of bread and milk, with more bread as accompaniment. A sunflower, a plant native to the Americas, brightens a dark corner of the Dutch courtyard.

Porridge has always played an important role in Dutch family and institutional menus. The orphans in the Amsterdam Municipal Orphanage were given porridge as the evening meal. Some days it was made from rice, groats, or barley; on other days it might be rye or wheat bread cooked with buttermilk, or bread and treacle cooked together with milk (see "Dutch Foodways: An American Connection," page 17).

For the Dutch settlers of New Netherland it was, therefore, very easy to get used to the Native Americans' cornmeal mush, called sapaen. The Dutch cooked this porridge in the same way the Native Americans did, but poured milk or buttermilk on it as it was served. As late as the 1830s, sapaen was listed under the heading of "National Dishes" on a menu for the celebration of Saint Nicholas' Eve in Albany.

Porridges, milk puddings, and custards, with their mixtures of milk and eggs, were considered very healthy foods in the seventeenth century and still hold an appeal for the Dutch. Vla (a runny kind of custard) is now commercially bottled and served as a common dessert. A more elegant lemon custard recipe is found in De Verstandige Kock: "Take the juice from the lemons and the yolks of 8 eggs, but add only the white of 4, grate a white bread of half a stuyver, [2½ cents' worth] then [add] a pint of sweet milk and sugar proportionately, neither too vigorously nor too slow should it boil." See cookbook for modern recipe.   PGR

133

53 Harmen van Steenwijck (1612–c. 1655)
Stoneware Jug, Game, and Fish

Dutch, 1646

oil on panel; 15¾ x 18¾ inches

signed and dated lower left: "H Steenwijck 1646"

Teresa Heinz and the late Senator John Heinz

COOKING UTENSILS, storage containers, and foodstuffs are heaped on a rustic wooden table. A dark cloth spills over the top of a small wooden tub supporting a large brass kettle. The cloth is caught beneath a yellow glazed earthenware porringer filled with perch and rock bass.

A snipe, its long neck dangling over the table's edge, draws attention to the crimped and fluted porringer handle. A lead-glazed earthenware pipkin lies on its side, its base and tripod feet showing charcoal smudges. A black bird with speckled breast and wings lies in its shadow. A quince and an apple, leaves still attached, sit on the table edge. An artichoke's spiky, open petals are visible against a small stoneware mug. The center of interest is a bulbous gray Frechen stoneware jug with a narrow neck and domed pewter lid. Heaped behind the jug, near the wooden tub and kettle, are another game bird and a rabbit.

Clearly, Harmen van Steenwijck was fascinated with the objects displayed here, attending to the textures of fur, leaves, feathers, skin, stoneware, and pewter, and the contrasting shapes of the pipkin, jug, and rabbit's ear. The potter's thumbprints are almost visible on the porringer. Even the cut marks on the table have been noted. The composition features a pale diagonal shaft of light, which glints on the metallic surfaces of the kettle and pewter lid, the silvery fish, the pipkin, the mug handle, and the fruit skins. Within this pyramidal arrangement, curving lines abound. In the tradition of monochrome still lifes, Steenwijck has used a very limited range of color.

This picture, unlike *pronk* still lifes, does not bespeak luxury, but rather commonplace foods and utensils. Dutch viewers could well appreciate its quiet dignity. Even the rabbit, which might have been poached by a peasant farmer, does not suggest the privileges reserved to the hunt. The only luxury item here is the artichoke, and it does not occupy a prominent space, but instead provides the artist with an opportunity to display his command of texture, line, and chiaroscuro shadows.   DRB

THE BRASS KETTLE on the left is unusual, because it has feet to allow it to stand over coals. Generally, kettles like this one had round bottoms and a bail handle for hanging over the fire. Used to boil water or foods in liquid, they were often made from brass, but because brass is poisonous, they were tinned on the inside. Round-bottomed kettles were used as trade goods in New Netherland. In 1677, for example, a group of Huguenot families bought about forty thousand acres in what is now New Paltz, New York, from the Esopus Indians, paying with an assortment of items, among them forty kettles, ten large and thirty small. Many remnants of kettles have also been found in Native American graves.

The cook might have used the kettle to prepare the perch and bass, displayed in the shallow bowl, in rapidly boiling salted water with parsley, dishing it up with cooking liquid for dunking (see cat. 22). Rabbits would have been boiled in a kettle as well, as the recipe below indicates. In the Middle Ages rabbits were among the small game hunted by the nobility, but gradually they became more widely available. Rabbits were also known in New Netherland. *Konijnen Eylandt* (Coney Island) was named for them by the Dutch settlers.

De Verstandige Kock suggests to prepare rabbits as follows: "Boil the rabbits whole in clean water with some salt, skim them clean, carve them and fry them in some butter in the pan until they turn red [reddish brown], then add a sauce of butter and some vinegar and sugar. Stir this together in the pan that it becomes a thick little sauce and pour it then over the rabbits. It tastes all right." Actually it tastes quite good. See cookbook for modern recipe.   PGR

54 Harmen van Steenwijck (1612–c. 1655)
Skillet and Game

Dutch, 1646

oil on panel; 15¾ x 18¾ inches

signed and dated: "H Steenwijk 1646"

Teresa Heinz and the late Senator John Heinz

A WIDE GOLDEN BAND of light streams diagonally across the picture from the upper left, illuminating cooking pots and game birds arranged on a hinged, wooden table. At the left corner, a water *snip* (snipe) lies on its back, its skinny legs hanging over the table's edge, and its needle-like beak pointing upward. Its feathers catch some of the light.

Toward the front is an overturned earthenware dish, projecting over the table's edge. A slight chip on the rim bespeaks use. Resting atop it is an overturned, partially glazed earthenware pipkin, its three legs smudged with soot. Crowded against the pipkin is the head of a plucked bean goose, its red beak casting a shadow. The breast skin shows remnants of quills and a red line of blood, but its wing and head feathers are intact. An empty German stoneware storage jug impressed with three medallions lies on its side. A wooden box supports three more game birds, a quince, and a lemon. A branch of lemon leaves is placed above a flat-lidded tripod iron baking pan.

Again, Harmen van Steenwijck has created a quiet, elegant still life using the modest utensils of ordinary daily life. No doubt such images were comforting to viewers, who could appreciate his subtle use of familiar objects, never repeated in precisely the same way, just as they could appreciate his subtle coloration and masterful use of both light and curving lines. Might viewers think of life's fleeting qualities as they considered the dead game birds and worn cookware? Or would they lick their lips, anticipating the tasty game bird dishes that could be created with these ingredients?

Today's viewers will note that the snipe and pipkin are also present in the other Steenwijck still life from the Heinz collection (see cat. 53). Since both are dated 1646, they may have been painted as companion pieces. Interestingly, in signing this painting, Harmen spelled his last name differently, here favoring *Steenwijk*.   DRB

JUST AS THE FLOWERS depicted in the floral still lifes actually bloom in different seasons, the birds in this painting are not seen at the same time of the year. The water snipe breeds in the Netherlands but migrates in winter, like the two "summer" teal shown. In contrast, the bean goose in the foreground winters but does not breed there. Both snipe and teal were cooked only partially eviscerated, or "met het drekje" (containing some dung), and considered a delicacy that way. The wild goose was spit-roasted and basted frequently with butter.

Dutch settlers in New Netherland marveled at the amount of waterfowl found in the new land. Adriaen van der Donck was quite lyrical in describing them, particularly swans: "[T]he bays and shores where they resort appear as if they were dressed in white drapery" (1968).

It is not only the foodstuffs that are of interest in this painting. The lid with a standing rim, covering the footed pan in the background of the painting, belongs to a Dutch oven, a name now given to any large casserole dish with a fitted cover. Dutch ovens were set over hot coals in the fireplace with additional coals heaped on top to create a small self-contained oven. Dutch ovens were used for baking *taert*, for which there are five recipes in the cookbook, or *pastey*, for which there are two recipes (see cookbook). The Dutch oven remained in use until the nineteenth century when stoves with ovens came into fashion.

Here is a recipe for a sweet spring chicken *pastey* from De *Verstandige Kock* that would have been baked in a Dutch oven. "Take the spring chicken boiled a little while, place it in the pastey, spice it with cinnamon, cloves, a little nutmeg, and ginger, place with it Damson prunes, candied pears and cherries, citron, pine nuts, and butter; let it bake for an hour. The sauce should be made with wine and sugar." See cookbook for modern recipe.   PGR

55 Harmen van Steenwijck (1612–c. 1655)
A Stoneware Jug, Fruit, and Dead Game Birds

Dutch, c. 1650s
oil on panel; 30¾ x 40⅛ inches
signed (middle right on box): "H. v. Steenwijck"
Private collection

ON A TABLE, partially draped with a dark blue cloth, a twig of red cherries, a few gooseberries, and a stem of black currants are arranged near the octagonal shaft of a *pasglas*, half filled with beer. In front of the beer glass are two dead songbirds. A branch of peaches is nestled amidst an exuberant profusion of red and white grapes on the vine, their spiraling tendrils reaching out to the glass. A stamped Rhineland salt-glazed jug stands atop a wooden box, which bears the artist's signature on its lid. The carcass of a partridge marked with blood red spots of plumage rests on the tablecloth in front of two pears. The picture is suffused with a soft light entering on a diagonal from the left. Light delineates the contours of the glass and jug, glistens on the skins of the fruits, and reflects off the partridge's feathers.

Steenwijck used pastel colors of pale yellow, pink, blue, and gray to provide a neutral backdrop for the featured items. The bird's red head and the yellow-skinned pears arranged on the blue cloth show his masterfully subtle manipulation of primary colors. He also exhibits linear mastery here. The bunch of cherries falling over the table's edge presages the cascading array of peaches and grapes. The gentle curves of the bird's wings are repeated in the fruit tree leaves, just as the bulbous shape of the pears is echoed by the stoneware jug.

Highly perishable white peaches and grapes were luxury fruits, and their presence in such profusion bespeaks wealth and plenty. The juxtaposition of these delicacies with beer, the drink of the masses, is another masterful touch, both visually and iconographically, and may have quietly reminded Steenwijck's viewers to take pleasure in ordinary beverages and foodstuffs. Others might have reacted to the erotic associations attributed to partridges in Caesar Ripa's *Iconologia* and have come to quite a different reading of this still life. DRB

PEACHES, PEARS, berries, and cherries were only some of the fruits cultivated in Dutch country house gardens. The wealthy burghers who could afford such homes would compete with their neighbors over the largest, best, or earliest fruits and plants. On a nice summer's afternoon they might invite each other to enjoy a glass of wine served with fruits and nuts from their gardens.

Dutch seeds and tree stock were also sent to New Netherland, where they grew abundantly. Various contemporary accounts describe the profusion of peach trees there bearing plentiful fruit. A 1639 inventory mentions an orchard of forty peach trees and fifteen grapevines. The cookbook contains recipes for cherry fruit leather and peaches in syrup. It also has one for a *pastey* that originally would have contained finches like the one on the left of the painting but has been modernized to use boned quail instead.

One can almost smell the ripe pears in the painting, ready to become part of a pear *taert*. Here is the recipe from *De Verstandige Kock*: "Take 12 of the tastiest, peeled pears, currants and sugar of each a quarter pound, 6 loot [1 loot equals 14 grams] butter, ginger, cinnamon of each a half loot in a crust . . . " See cookbook for modern recipe. PGR

56 Abraham Susenier (c. 1620–before 1672)
Still Life with a Lobster, Roemer, Oysters, Grapes, and a Knife

Dutch, 1660s
oil on canvas; 15¼ x 19¾ inches
Lawrence Steigrad Fine Arts

A BRILLIANT RED, cooked lobster is arranged on the lower ledge next to one open and two closed oysters. Grapes are heaped on the ledge behind the vermilion crustacean, their tendrils and vine leaves gleaming against the dark background. A knife with an ivory handle, a raspberry-prunted *roemer* filled with white wine, and an oyster opened on the half shell are on the upper ledge. Droplets of the oyster's liquor have fallen onto the ledge.

The lobster dominates this picture, making it akin to a portrait study, with the same careful attention paid to its pincer claws, antennae, gleaming black eye, tufted, jointed swimmerettes, carapace cracks, and curled, segmented tail as other painters might give to the features of human beings. This man knew his lobsters!

Roemers are featured in many still-life pictures, but here one can almost feel the knobby texture of the prunts and the coils of the glass base. The pulsing dark organs of the oysters are also splendidly captured. The inner sheen of the oyster shells reveals not only the smooth, nacreous lining but also the laminated ridges of their outer edges, which attract the viewer's eyes and the eater's fingers.

Many elaborate banquet still lifes by Dutch and Flemish painters include lobsters along with their luxury foods and costly tableware, as in Clara Peeters's and Michiel Simons's pictures (see cats. 40 and 48). However, Susenier's focus on the anatomy of this crustacean represents a significant departure from that usual practice. Here the lobster is the star.

The flesh from a cooked lobster, like the one used by Susenier as a model, would have begun to decay long before the artist finished sketching or painting it. Whether he was working in the cold of winter or the heat of summer, he would have had to steel himself against the stench when closely examining its structure.

Because they require a rocky sea bottom to live, lobsters were not fished off the sandy Dutch coast in the province of Holland, although some were available from the coastal province of Zeeland. As a result, fresh lobsters—for painters or banquet diners—were not easily acquired and were rarely sold in Dutch fish markets.   DRB

THE LOBSTERS on both sides of the North Atlantic are very similar. However, slight variations have led to their classification as two different species, with the American lobster (*Homarus Americanus*) being the larger of the two. Many Americans erroneously assume that European lobsters do not have claws. However, only the spiny lobsters, such as the Mediterranean *Palinurus elephas* of the warmer waters, lack claws.

While the colors of the shells range from dark blue to green according to habitat, lobsters turn a vivid red when cooked, as depicted in the Susenier painting. *De Verstandige Kock* tells how to do it: "Take water, vinegar, salt, and pepper-powder, let it cook well together [let it come to a rolling boil], add the lobster. . . . It will have beautiful color." This recipe does not need a modern adaptation.   PGR

57 Constantijn Verhout (active 1662–1667)
Portrait of Cornelis Abrahamsz. Graswinckel (1582–1664) (?), the Delft Brewer

Dutch, 1662
oil on panel; 13¼ x 10⅞ inches
signed and dated (lower left): "C Verhout 1662"
Isabel and Alfred Bader

THIS CONTEMPLATIVE STUDY of a Delft brewer also features a number of his prized but modest possessions, all carefully delineated. Indicative of his trade, the man holds a Westerwald stoneware beer jug, known as a *krug* in German, in both hands. Although his eyes are cast downward, the brewer is not actually looking at the drink, but is caught in a moment of reflection, perhaps considering the decline in the demand and price for beer in Delft during the 1660s?

His ladderback chair is positioned next to a table, where a white clay pipe rests near his elbow. An earthenware tripod bowl holds a wooden spoon. A candlesnuffer, a metal frying pan, and a brush hang suspended on the wall. Above these items is a wooden shelf containing household debris: two books, a leather pail, a pair of slippers, and a spouted jug with a broken handle. Above his head with its fur-trimmed hat, a wooden splint sieve is mounted on the wall.

Based on similarities to a portrait in the *Hofje van Gratie* (a charity home for aged women, long supported by the Graswinckel family), it is assumed that the sitter is Cornelis Abrahamsz. Graswinckel, a member of a prominent Delft family who also served as the *kerkmeester* (church warden) for both the *Oude Kerk* (Old Church) and *Nieuwe Kerk* (New Church) in Delft. If the sitter is Graswinckel, he has permitted the portrait painter to depict him in a highly unconventional way: as a simple man in a rather plain interior rather than as an elegantly attired important community leader.

An old man looking into a beer jug, or holding one in his hands, figures in other Dutch artists' imagery, but usually as a *kannekijker* (literally, "jug-looker") functioning as a comic drunk, even when included in allegories on the sense of sight. Paintings by Verhout are exceedingly rare. The only other painting whose attribution is certain is a picture of a young scholar asleep behind a pile of books, signed "C. Verhout, 1663" (Nationalmuseum, Stockholm).   DRB

THE FRYING PAN with sloping sides, hanging on the back wall, is called a *pannekoeckenpan* (pancake pan), ideally suited for making pancakes. Ships' records show that cookware, including pans and frying pans like this, were exported to New Netherland. As discussed elsewhere (see cats. 41 and 50), the lower classes as well as the rich middle class of the seventeenth-century Netherlands enjoyed pancakes. Since it was such a popular food, it is no wonder that when the Dutch settled in New Netherland, they adapted local foodstuffs to a familiar preparation, using their customary recipes (see cookbook), but also incorporating native foodstuffs. For example, they mashed cooked pumpkin and mixed it with cornmeal to make pancakes. A modern recipe, featuring these two main ingredients, can be found in the cookbook.   PGR

58 Abraham Willemsen (or Willemsens) (c. 1610–1672)
The Milk Vendor

Flemish, c. 1655–1660

oil on canvas; 34 x 45½ inches

New Orleans Museum of Art; bequest of Bert Piso, 81.267

ON THE GROUNDS of a rural farm house milking time is over. A man dressed in a red jacket, dark blue cap and leggings, and brown breeches, with a white cloth apron wrapped around his waist, pours the contents of a bucket into a brass milk jug held by a kneeling customer. She is dressed in a white cap and blouse, dark bodice and apron, and a brilliant red skirt. Her sleeves are rolled up, revealing strong arms capable of hefting her heavy load. A ragged-looking barefoot beggar boy, leaning on his walking stick, beseechingly holds out a small bowl hoping for milk. A young girl emerges from the doorway of the building, holding a wide pan.

Animals fill the courtyard, including three white geese, a couple of hens, a strutting cockerel, several other domestic birds, and pigeons. A dovecote is positioned on the roof of the barn. There are also two sheep and a horned ram near the saddled burro. An old broom, wicker basket, wagon wheel, and redware platter are lying on the ground near the wooden fence. A woman (with a milk can balanced on her head and basket over her arm) and a small child enter the courtyard through a gateway. In the background rolling fields are silhouetted against a pink and blue Italianate sky.

Willemsen's chubby-cheeked farmwomen and children appear in several pictures attributed to him, and a quiet mood pervades his work, almost as if the staffage was arrested in time and motion.

Dutch picture owners apparently enjoyed landscapes of the Italian countryside, marine views of Italian ports, or animated scenes of Italian markets, for these overarching themes are found in many works created by Netherlandish painters. They also appreciated the unfamiliar lighting effects of the southern sun; the undulating terrain, so different from Holland's flat polder lands; the presence of farm animals, like burros and goats, not native to the Dutch Republic; and costumes and facial characteristics different from those found in the Low Countries. Exotic, yes, and yet somehow familiar. DRB

IN THIS GENRE SCENE, the woman holds a piece of cheese-cloth used for filtering the milk that the vendor is pouring into her brass pitcher. Milk was the chief ingredient for butter and cheese making as well as for cooking and was used less for drinking, although the boy standing next to her would like some for that purpose (see cats. 47 and 52). However, Dutch physician Stefanus Blankaart asserted, "In milk you have butter, cheese and whey, which is food and drink together and not nearly as unhealthy as some assume" (1633). Milk with or without cream, buttermilk, curdled milk, and cream by itself, were used for a variety of dishes. As breeding procedures became more sophisticated, milk production increased and more recipes for milk dishes, such as porridges and custards, subsequently appeared in period cookbooks.

Cows grazing on pastures of clay soil produce milk that tastes different from the milk of cows grazing on pastures of a peaty or sandy soil. This in turn affects the end product of cheese or butter. The milk and butter of New Netherland must, therefore, have tasted different from those of the homeland.

The recipes from *De Verstandige Kock* for pancakes, *olie-koecken*, and custards—typical of the foods eaten at the time—and their modern versions in our cookbook, all employ various quantities of milk. PGR

59 Emanuel de Witte (c. 1616–c. 1691)
The New Fish Market in Amsterdam

Dutch, 1678

oil on canvas; 17½ x 20½ inches

signed and dated at lower left (below the stork): "E. De. Witte Ao 1678"

Wadsworth Atheneum Museum of Art; The Ella Gallup Sumner and Mary Catlin Sumner Collection Fund, 1949.447

WHILE FISHWIVES and fishmongers interact with other customers, a woman and her child approach the New Fish Market in Amsterdam where saltwater fish was sold. The brass shopping can on her arm indicates the woman's intention to buy food from one of the stalls. At far left, a long-legged stork, attracted to the market by small fish or discarded fish guts, pecks at food on the brick pavement.

The mother has a large white collar arranged over her rose jacket and a clean white apron tied over her skirt, protecting it from the dirt of the market place. A dark scarf covers her hair. The ribbons on her sleeves and the bodice of her jacket indicate her prosperity. Her son is dressed in a white shirt, dark jacket, and hat.

The rooflines of many buildings surrounding the fish market are visible at right. Incongruously, the large sails of an ocean-going vessel are depicted here, as if it were docked nearby; this was impossible, since ships this big could not get through the locks and canals of Amsterdam, but were offloaded in the Zuiderzee or River IJ. The Jan Rodenspoort Tower shown in the distance is also not properly situated.

Emanuel de Witte, best remembered for his paintings of church interiors, is known to have created at least seven fish market scenes beginning in the early 1650s, when he left Delft to work in Amsterdam. Fish markets were a popular theme in Dutch paintings. Women shopping at markets with their children symbolized at least two of a wife's duties. As well as feeding their families, they (or sometimes servants) taught both boys and girls how to recognize and select good, fresh, wholesome foods.

Were De Witte's patrons taken by the nurturing possibility implicit in this picture? Might some have wondered about the time of day and weather conditions that afforded such an unusual color-streaked sky? Or would they have been amused by the liberties the artist took with the topography? Did they remember that his church interiors were also painterly constructions, not architectural renderings?

DRB

AS WAS THE CASE for other important foodstuffs, such as bread and meat, the processing and marketing of fish was strictly regulated by the government, thereby ensuring a superior product. In addition, fishmongers were members of the Saint Peter's Guild, which had its own set of regulations.

The Amsterdam fish market was divided into two parts. One area was for the sale of saltwater fish, such as salmon, cod, turbot, haddock, flounder, plaice, thornback (ray), and, of course, herring. *Stokvis* (dried salted cod) was also available, and fried fish was sold in nearby stalls. The other part of the market sold river fish, such as pike, eel, perch, bass, and bream (see cats. 22, 36, and 53).

In keeping with this tradition, the following recipes from *De Verstandige Kock* feature both salt- and freshwater fish: "To stew salmon in a different manner: Remove the scales of the salmon, wash it clean, take a little tin bowl of water and a little bowl of wine-vinegar for each slice of salmon, grate a piece of wheat bread and some whole pepper, half a nutmeg, a little crushed mace, no salt. Place these in a flat [shallow earthenware] pot, let it stew together, add a little butter to it after it has stewed a while."

"To boil a pike in the Spanish manner: Take a lemon, cut it in slices, place them in a little pot with some Rhenish wine, water, butter, ginger, saffron, and cloves, let it stew together until it is [done] enough, then pour it on a platter and place the boiled pike in it." Modern versions of both recipes can be found in the cookbook.

PGR

147

60 Peter Wtewael (1596–1660)

Kitchen Scene

Dutch, c. 1625–1628

oil on canvas; 44¾ x 63 inches

The Metropolitan Museum of Art; Rogers Fund, 1906. (06.288)

A TANNED PEASANT MAN pauses to joke with a maid in this kitchen scene. He holds a dead game bird in one hand, and has a basket of eggs over the other arm while also grasping an earthenware jug. The plump kitchen maid is spitting a rack of meat and a plucked bird. She appears slightly older than her companion and smiles knowingly at him.

A wooden table holds a flayed sheep's head, roasted meat, dead rabbits and snipes, a brass skimmer, a mortar and pestle, a knife, a ball of string, and a wooden tub. A dead cockerel hangs above it. A brass cooking pot is stored on the wooden shelf. In the background is another shelf of pewter plates, with earthenware wine ewers hanging below.

At first glance, the viewer sees a well-stocked kitchen with food preparation under way. Upon closer examination, one may recognize the sexual allusions. The dead bird held by the peasant man may be an invitation to "bird" or to have sex; the man's finger points suggestively in a then-and-now lewd gesture implying sexual intercourse. The womb-shaped earthenware jug, with its open lid, suggests that the maid is not a virgin and may accept, or at least not take offense at, his invitation. Her spitting of the meats also has lascivious implications, as does the grinding movement of the pestle in the mortar. Eggs were associated with sexual activity too, alluding both to fertility and to testicles. Except for the viewer, all the other "witnesses" to this exchange—rabbits, rooster, birds, and sheep—are dead and unseeing. Has Wtewael invited voyeurs to share the joke?

The erotically charged theme of peasant men, market vendors, or hunters presenting women with game birds occurs in many Dutch pictures. The artist's father, Joachim, depicted a man with an egg basket moving his hand under the skirt of a kitchen maid. No doubt, father and son both knew that *kip* ("chicken") was also Dutch slang for a loose woman.

Stories were "told" about Dutch kitchens by painters. Certainly there was no lack of gossip, bawdy songs, or theatrical farces about mischief cooked up between the kitchen maid and the man of the house, or between the scullery maid and a peddler who came to the kitchen door. Popular folk wisdom suggests that not only onions produced tears in the kitchen.   DRB

THE RIBS AND FOWL that the maid is about to put on the spit will be roasted over the fire. The other meats will be cooked in stews, used for broth, or baked in savory raised pies, while the eggs, fresh from the hen house, will be used in custards, pastries, and pancakes, or "stirred" with smoked meat, as one of the recipes in De Verstandige Kock suggests.

Anne Stevenson van Cortlandt (1774–1821) of Albany had a not-to-be-missed variation of the De Verstandige Kock recipe in her handwritten cookbook. She combined mushrooms, herbs, and eggs beaten with orange juice and red wine to create a scrumptious version of scrambled eggs called Mushroom Fricasie. Mushrooms were available on both sides of the Atlantic. Two editions of De Verstandige Kock, printed in Antwerp, contained a separate chapter on fungi. These were the first recorded mushroom recipes in the Netherlands. They were written by Frans van Sterbeeck, an expert in the field, who later became the first author to write a scientific work on the subject. Here is Anne Stevenson van Cortlandt's excellent recipe from her handwritten cookbook: "Stew them and pour away the liquor, fry them with a little butter and onion. Shred small some sweet marjorum and Thyme stript from the stalk. Season it with salt and pepper. Make a sauce of eggs beat in with the juice of orange, claret, the gravy of a legg of mutton & nutmegg. Shake them well; give them a few tosses in the pan. Put them in a dish rubbed with shallots, garnished with lemon or orange" (n.d.). See cookbook for modern recipe.   PGR

GLOSSARY

akeleipokal: (German) "grape cup"

ananas van Brasiliaenschen stam: pineapple of Brazilian origin

appel: apple

artisocken onder de aert: literally "artichokes under the earth"; Jerusalem artichokes

bakermat: long, low basket, long enough to accommodate a woman seated with outstretched legs

banketje: literally "little banquet"; a still life displaying an elaborate arrangement of expensive foods and serving pieces

bekerschroef: literally "goblet screw"; gilt goblet holder

berkemeier: wine glass

beschuit: rusks

bokaal: an ornate gilt glass or cup

bokaaldeksel: a domed cover for a *bokaal*

bordeeltje: a little bordello; bordello scene

brandewijnkom: two-handled silver-paneled bowl for brandy

brandje: little fire; fire scene

brokken: pieces

burgerlijk: middle class; bourgeois

carsteling: a regional term (in Gouda) for the bowl-shaped pastry more commonly known as *zottinnekoecken*

condale: Anglicized phonetic spelling of *kandeel*; see below

coortegardje: guardroom scene

cruller: now donut; originally crisp, deep-fried corkscrew-curled pastry

Deventer koek: a type of spice cake originating in the town of Deventer

doelen: practice ranges for guns and crossbows

doopvis: fish for dunking

doot coeckjes: funeral cookies

duivekater: a large flat bread shaped like a shinbone or diamond and baked during the holiday season from early December through the New Year

duivel: the devil

eierschotel: a regional term (in Friesland) for the bowl-shaped pastry more commonly known as *zottinekoeck*

Enghalskrug: (German) a narrow-necked stoneware jug

façon de Venise: (French) literally "in the style of Venice"; Venetian style

fruytje: literally "little fruit"; a still life featuring fruit displayed in goblets, dishes, or baskets

genever: Holland's gin

girasole: a plant with flowers that follow the sun

glasbokaal: covered glass wine decanter or covered goblet

hammetje: literally "little ham"; a still life with ham prominently displayed

herenbrood: "gentlemen's bread" or white bread

hutspot: hodgepodge or hotchpotch; a one-pot dish of chopped meats and vegetables

karnton: wooden butter churn

kandeel: spiced wine with eggs; the customary drink celebrating the birth of a child

kannekijker: literally "jug-looker"; tippler, sot, or drunkard

kater: tomcat

kerkmeester: church warden

kermis: carnival, street fair

kinderstoel: infant's high chair

kindervriend: literally "children's friend"; a term for St. Nicholas

kinnebacks-hammetje: little jawbone ham

kip: chicken; slang term for a loose woman

kleine banck van justitie: an inferior bench of judicature

kluchtspelen: bawdy comedies or farces

koek: flat, not highly risen, cake

koekepan: pancake pan

koekje: cookie; diminutive of *koek*; seventeenth-century Dutch variations included *koeckjens* or *koecxkens*; also small items fried in a pan or small sweet morsels, such as candied quince squares

koeldranken: cooling drinks

kolder: a buffalo hide sleeveless jerkin

koolsla: cabbage salad; now coleslaw

kraamkamer: special birthing room

krakelingen: sweet pretzels

krug: (German) stoneware beer jug

krullen: literally "curls"; a curl-shaped deep-fried pastry; variations: *crulla, crullar, cruller*

kunstkamer: art collection room

luiermandkast: layette cupboard

maandbloeyers: ; literally "month-bloomers"; wild strawberries

maneschijntje: literally "little moon shine"; moonlight scene

meisje: girl or young woman

met het drekje: containing some dung

Miles Christianus: Knight of Christ

musico: inn for playing or listening to music, and for dancing

nagel: clove; nail

nieuwjaarskoeken: thin, crisp wafers or cookies, served on New Year's Day

Noordzee krab: the common crab of western and northern Europe

olie-koecken: literally "oil-cakes"; deep-fried balls of dough with raisins, apples, and almonds that became a forerunner of the donut; variations on the word include *oelykoeks, ollykoeks, ole cook,* and *oly cook*

oliebollen: literally "oil-balls"; modern name for *olie-koecken*

olipodrigo: an elaborate stew

ontbijtje: literally "little breakfast"; a still life depicting simple foodstuffs

pannekoeckenpan: pancake pan

pasglas: a clear cylindrical glass with dark-colored coils marking measures

pastey backer: pastry baker (especially of raised pies); often the town's caterer

pastey: savory raised pie

Pinksterblom: Pinkster (Pentecost) flower

plooischotel: a lobed bowl or serving platter

poffen-broodt: small pancakes

poffertjes: puffed silver dollar pancakes

pompoen: pumpkin

primeur: the first vegetable(s) of a particular season

pronk: ornately luxurious, even showy or ostentatious

puntschotel: pointed silver presentation tray

quaasiens: summer squash

quee-koeckjes: candied quince squares

rijding: variable weight

roemer: inexpensive drinking glass with round bowl and footed stem

sabot: clog

sapaen: cornmeal mush

schootjes: portioned rolls

schout: sheriff

schuilkerken: hidden churches for Roman Catholics

sewant or seewant: wampum

snip: snipe

stadhouder: political steward; national or provincial government head

stilleven: still-life paintings

stokvis: dried salted cod

stoof: a foot warmer containing a pipkin with hot coals

stuyver: five cents' worth

suikertjes: sugar candies or comfits

tabagie: a smoking saloon

tabakje: literally "little tobacco"; a still life featuring the paraphenalia of smoking, including tobacco pipes, smoldering hemp wicks and wooden splinters with sulfer used to light tobacco pipes

taert: sweet raised pie

taertpanne: Dutch oven

tazza: shallow, wide-mouthed, footed drinking goblet or compote dish usually made of precious metal, glass, or porcelain

theerandjes: literally "tea edges"; strips made from a clove-flavored dough, topped with candied orange peel and citron

topos: a conventional symbol or visual metaphor

trekschuit: canal boat

tric trac: a form of backgammon

tronie: amusing or grotesque, portrait-like character study

tussen twee schotels: between two dishes

valhoedje: a child's protective bumper hat

vanitas: reminder of fleeting earthly pleasures and sensory delights

verjuice: juice from unripe grapes or apples

vierendeel: quarter

vla: a runny kind of custard

vleeschkuyp: a wooden preserving tub for pickling meat

vleugelglas: winged glass

vuurmand: a dome-shaped device to dry diapers

wafels (pronounced "wafuls"): waffles

zalet-juffers: high-priced courtesans

zeebeschuit: literally "sea biscuit"; hardtack

zetting: variable price

zottinnekoecken: literally "crazy woman's cakes"; an airy pastry akin to rusks

zwavelstokjen: wooden splinters with sulfur used to light tobacco pipes

PHRASES OR SAYINGS

"Alte veel is ongesont": Too much is unhealthy

"Caseum habens non eget obsonio": He who has cheese does not need dessert

"Gelijck men handelt den meloen, soo moet men oock met vrienden doen": The way you choose a melon, you should choose your friends

"In de rommelingh ist vet": In the commotion [of churning] comes the fat

"Vanitas, vanitas, omnia est vanitas": (Latin) Vanity, vanity, all is vanity

"Vroeg rijp, vroeg rot": Early ripe, early rot

CITED AND SUGGESTED WORKS

This list covers works cited both in this volume and in the supplementary cookbook

SEVENTEENTH-CENTURY DUTCH ART

Ackley, Clifford S. 1980. *Printmaking in the Age of Rembrandt.* Boston: Museum of Fine Arts.

Alpers, Svetlana. 1983. *The Art of Describing: Dutch Art in the Seventeenth Century.* Chicago: Univ. of Chicago Press.

Brown, Christopher. 1984. *Images of a Golden Past: Dutch Genre Painting of the Seventeenth Century.* New York: Abbeville Press.

———. 1999. *Scenes of Everyday Life: Dutch Genre Paintings from the Mauritshuis Collection.* Oxford: Ashmolean Museum.

Caffin, Charles H. 1909. *The Story of Dutch Painting.* New York: Century Company.

Chong, Alan, and Wouter Kloek. 1999. *Still-Life Paintings from the Netherlands, 1550–1720.* English-language version edited by Barbara J. Bradley. Zwolle: Waanders Publishers in cooperation with Rijksmuseum, Amsterdam, and the Cleveland Museum of Art.

De Jongh, Eddy, and Ger Luijten. 1997. *Mirror of Everyday Life: Genreprints in the Netherlands, 1550–1700.* Translated by Michael Hoyle. Ghent: Snoeck-Ducaju & Zoon in cooperation with the Rijksmuseum, Amsterdam.

James, Henry. 1872. "The Metropolitan Museum's '1871 Purchase.'" *Atlantic Monthly* (June).

Johnson, John Graver. 1892. *A Sightseer in Berlin and Holland Among Pictures.* Philadelphia, n.p.

Kahr, Madlyn Millner. 1993. *Dutch Painting in the Seventeenth Century.* 2d. ed. New York: Harper Collins.

Kiers, Judike, and Fieke Tissink. 2000. *The Glory of the Golden Age: Painting, Sculpture, and Decorative Art.* Zwolle: Waanders in cooperation with the Rijksmuseum, Amsterdam.

Mandel, Oscar. 1996. *The Cheerfulness of Dutch Art: A Rescue Operation.* Doornspijk: Davaco.

Segal, Sam. 1989. *A Prosperous Past: The Sumptuous Still Life in the Netherlands, 1600–1700.* Edited by William B. Jordan, translated by P. M. van Tongeren. The Hague: SDU Publishers.

Slive, Seymour. 1995. *Dutch Painting, 1600–1800.* New Haven and London: Yale University Press.

Sutton, Peter C. 1984. *Masters of Seventeenth-Century Dutch Genre Painting.* Ed. Jane Iandola Watkins. Philadelphia: Philadelphia Museum of Art and Univ. of Pennsylvania Press.

Trumble, Alfred. 1899. *The Collector* 8 (April):1.

Westermann, Mariët. 1996. *A Worldly Art: The Dutch Republic, 1585–1718.* New York: Harry N. Abrams.

———. 2001. *Art & Home: Dutch Interiors in the Age of Rembrandt.* Zwolle: Waanders Publishers in cooperation with the Denver Art Museum and the Newark Museum.

THE NETHERLANDS OF THE SEVENTEENTH CENTURY

Aglionby, William. 1669. *The Present State of the United Provinces of the Low Countries.* London: n.p.

Cats, Jacob. 1632. *Spiegel van den Ouden en Nieuwen Tyt* (Mirror of old and new times]). The Hague: Isaac Burghoorn.

———. 1880. *Alle de Werken van Jacob Cats* (All the works of Jacob Cats). Edited by W. N. Wolterink. Dordrecht: J. P. Revers.

Deursen, A. Th. van, 1991. *Plain Lives in a Golden Age: Popular Culture, Religion, and Society in Seventeenth-Century Holland.* Trans. Maarten Ultee. Cambridge and New York: Cambridge Univ. Press.

Kistemaker, Renée, and Roelof van Gelder. 1983. *Amsterdam: The Golden Age, 1275–1795.* Trans. Paul Foulkes. New York: Abbeville Press.

Kistemaker, Renée, Michiel Wagenaar, and Jos van Assendelft. 1984. *Amsterdam Marktstad.* Amsterdam: Dienst van het Marktwezen.

Murris, Roelof. 1925. *La Hollande et les Hollandais du XVI au XVIIeme siecles, vus par le Francais.* Paris: n.p. Quoted in Schama, Simon. 1987. *The Embarrassment of Riches: An Interpretation of Dutch Culture in the Golden Age.* New York: Alfred A. Knopf, n.129.

North, Michael. 1997. *Art and Commerce in the Dutch Golden Age.* Trans. Catherine Hill. New Haven and London: Yale Univ. Press.

Regin, Deric. 1976. *Traders, Artists, Burghers: A Cultural History of Amsterdam in the Seventeenth Century.* Assen: Van Gorcum.

Schama, Simon. 1987. *The Embarrassment of Riches: An Interpretation of Dutch Culture in the Golden Age.* New York: Alfred A. Knopf.

Visscher, Roemer. 1614. *Sinnepoppen.* Amsterdam: Willem Iansz.

Zumthor, Paul. 1994. *Daily Life in Rembrandt's Holland.* Trans. Simon Watson Taylor. 1959, 1962. Reprint, Stanford: Stanford Univ. Press.

CULINARY HISTORY

B. G. 1763. *Volmaakte Onderrigtinge, ten dienst der Koek-Bakkers of hunne Leerlingen* (Perfect instructions to serve the pastry bakers, or their students). Wed J. van Egmont Op de Reguliers Bree-Straat.

Blankaart, Stephanus, M.D. 1633. *De Borgerlyke Tafel Om land gesond sonder ziekten te leven,* Amsterdam, n.p.

De Cierlijcke Voorsnijdinge Aller Tafel Gerechten. 1664. Amsterdam: Hieronymus Sweerts.

De Verstandige Kock (The sensible cook). 1683. In *Het Vermakelijck Landtleven* (The pleasurable country life). Amsterdam: Marcus Doornick.

Elting, Anna Maria. 1819. Handwritten cookbook, May 8. Archives, Huguenot Historical Society, New Paltz, New York.

Hasbrouck, Hylah. 1890. "Hylah Hasbrouck's Receipts" (handwritten cookbook). Archives, Huguenot Historical Society, New Paltz, New York.

Lefferts, Maria Lott. n.d. "Mrs. Lefferts Book" (handwritten cookbook). Archives, Lefferts House, Prospect Park Alliance, Brooklyn, New York.

Morse, Elizabeth Ann Breese. 1805. "Mrs. E. A. Morse, Her Book" (handwritten cookbook). April 10. Archives, Young-Morse Historic Site, Poughkeepsie, New York.

Peyster, Anna de. n.d. Handwritten cookbook. Archives, Historic Hudson Valley, Tarrytown, New York.

Riley, Gilian. 1994. *The Dutch Table*. Rohnert Park, CA: Pomegranate Artbooks.

Rose, Peter G. 1993. *Foods of the Hudson*. Woodstock: Overlook Press.

———. 1998. *The Sensible Cook: Dutch Foodways in the Old and the New World*. 1989. Reprint, Syracuse: Syracuse Univ. Press.

Schoonmaker, Jemima. n.d. Archives, Huguenot Historical Society, New Paltz, New York.

Tannahill, Reay. 1973. *Food in History*. New York: Stein and Day.

Van Cortlandt, Anne Stevenson. n.d. Handwritten cookbook. Archives, Historic Hudson Valley, Tarrytown, New York.

Van Rensselaer, Maria Sanders. n.d. Handwritten cookbook. Archives, Historic Cherry Hill, Albany, New York.

Vorselman, Gheeraert. [1560] 1971. *Eenen Nyeuwen Coock Boeck*. Annotated edition. Antwerp: Elly Cockx-Indestege, Wiesbaden Guido Pressler.

Wheaton, Barbara Ketcham. 1983. *Savoring the Past*. Philadelphia: Univ. of Pennsylvania Press.

NEW NETHERLAND HISTORY

For a more complete bibliography, please consult the New Netherland Project website: www.nnp.org.

Blackburn, Roderic H., and Ruth Piwonka, 1988. *Remembrance of Patria: Dutch Arts and Culture in Colonial America, 1609–1776*. Albany: Albany Institute of History & Art.

Bronck, Widow. 1648. Inventory. "Register of the Provincial Secretary, 1642–1647." Vol. 2 of *New York Historical Manuscripts: Dutch*. New York State Archives.

Burke, Tomas E., Jr. 1991. *Mohawk Frontier: The Dutch Community of Schenectady, New York, 1661–1710*. Ithaca: Cornell Univ. Press.

Cohen, David Steven. 1992. *The Dutch-American Farm*. New York: New York Univ. Press.

Cornell, Jaray, ed. 1968. *Historic Chronicles of New Amsterdam: Colonial New York and Early Long Island*. Port Washington, New York: Ira J. Friedman. Quoting Charles Wooley.

Danckaerts, Jasper. 1913. *Journal of Jasper Danckaerts, 1679–1680*. Ed. Barlett Burleigh James and J. Franklin Jameson. New York: Charles Scribner's Sons.

Goodfriend, Joyce D. 1992. *Before the Melting Pot: Society and Culture in Colonial New York City, 1664–1730*. Princeton: Princeton Univ. Press.

Grant, Anne Macvicar. 1809. *Memoirs of an American Lady: with Sketches of Manners and Scenery in America, as They Existed Previous to the Revolution*. New York: Samuel Campbell.

Groft, Tammis K., and Mary Alice Mackay, eds. 1998. *Albany Institute of History & Art: Two Hundred Years of Collecting*. New York: Hudson Hills Press.

Hamilton, Alexander. 1907. *Hamilton's "Itinerarium . . . 1774."* Edited by Albert Bushnell Hart. St. Louis: privately printed by William K. Bixby.

Kalm, Peter. 1987. *Travels in North America: The English Version of 1770*. New York: Dover Publications.

Kenney, Alice P. 1989. *Stubborn for Liberty: The Dutch in New York*. 1975. Reprint, Syracuse: Syracuse Univ. Press.

Lott, Abraham. 1870. "A Journal of a Voyage to Albany, Etc., Made by Abraham Lott, Treasurer of the Colony of New York 1774." *The Historical Magazine* 8 (Second Series), no. 2 (August):65-74.

Meeske, Harrison. 1998. *The Hudson Valley Dutch and Their Houses*. Fleischmanns, NY: Purple Mountain Press.

Murphy, Henry C. 1861. *A Memoir of the First Poet in New Netherland, with his Poems desciptive of the Colony*. The Hague, n.p. Quoting Jacob Steendam.

Nissenson, Samuel G. 1973. *The Patroon's Domain*. 1937. Reprint, New York: Columbia Univ. Press.

Paige, Harriet Bowers Mumford. c. 1860. "Eight handwritten journals: Entries and observations on the Schenectady community, c.1860." Schenectady County Historical Society.

Rink, Oliver A. 1986. *Holland on the Hudson: An Economic and Social History of Dutch People*. Ithaca, Cornell Univ. Press.

Stayton, Kevin L. 1990. *Dutch by Design: Traditions and Change in Two Historic Houses*. New York: Brooklyn Museum.

Trelease, Allen W. 1960. *Indian Affairs in Colonial New York: The Seventeenth Century*. Ithaca: Cornell Univ. Press.

Van der Donck, Adriaen. [1655] 1968. *A Description of the New Netherlands*. Syracuse: Syracuse Univ. Press.

Van Rensselaer, Jeremias. 1932. *Correspondence of Jeremias van Rensselaer, 1651–1674*. Ed. and trans. A. J. F. van Laer. Albany: Univ. of the State of New York.

Van Rensselaer, Maria. 1935. *Correspondence of Maria van Rensselaer, 1669–1689*. Ed. and trans. A. J. F. van Laer. Albany: Univ. of New York.

Wilcoxen, Charlotte. 1984. *Seventeenth Century Albany: A Dutch Profile*. 1981. Reprint, Albany: Albany Institute of History & Art.

———. 1987. *Dutch Trade and Ceramics in America in the Seventeenth Century*. Albany: Albany Institute of History & Art.

FURTHER READING

For those who wish to seek out Dutch paintings in American museum collections, the indispensable guide is Peter C. Sutton's *Dutch Art in America*, published in 1986 by the Netherlands—America Amity Trust in cooperation with Wm. B. Eerdmans in Grand Rapids, Michigan, and J. H. Kok in Kampen, the Netherlands.

INDEX